T0204735

James Franco

Other books in the People in the News series:

Maya Angelou
Tyra Banks
Glenn Beck
David Beckham
Beyoncé
Sandra Bullock
Fidel Castro
Kelly Clarkson
Hillary Clinton
Stephen Colbert
Suzanne Collins
Miley Cyrus
Ellen Degeneres
Johnny Depp
Hilary Duff
Zac Efron
Eminem
Brett Favre
Roger Federer
50 Cent
Glee Cast and Creators
Jeff Gordon
Al Gore
Tony Hawk
Salma Hayek
Jennifer Hudson
LeBron James
Jay-Z
Derek Jeter
Steve Jobs
Dwayne Johnson
Angelina Jolie
Jonas Brothers
Elena Kagan
Alicia Keys
Kim Jong Il

Coretta Scott King
Ashton Kutcher
Taylor Lautner
Spike Lee
Tobey Maguire
Eli Manning
John McCain
Stephenie Meyer
Barack Obama
Michelle Obama
Apolo Anton Ohno
Danica Patrick
Nancy Pelosi
Katy Perry
Tyler Perry
David Petraeus
Queen Latifah
Daniel Radcliffe
Condoleezza Rice
Rihanna
Alex Rodriguez
Derrick Rose
J.K. Rowling
Shakira
Tupac Shakur
Will Smith
Gwen Stefani
Ben Stiller
Hilary Swank
Taylor Swift
Justin Timberlake
Usher
Lindsey Vonn
Denzel Washington
Serena Williams
Oprah Winfrey

James Franco

By Christie Brewer Boyd

LUCENT BOOKS
A part of Gale, Cengage Learning

GALE
CENGAGE Learning·

Detroit • New York • San Francisco • New Haven, Conn • Waterville, Maine • London

Library of Congress Cataloging-in-Publication Data

Boyd, Christie Brewer.
  James Franco / by Christie Brewer Boyd.
    p. cm. -- (People in the news)
  Includes bibliographical references and index.
  ISBN 978-1-4205-0754-6 (hardcover)
1. Franco, James, 1978---Juvenile literature. 2. Actors--United
  States--Biography--Juvenile literature. I. Title.
  PN2287.F673B69 2013
  791.4302'8092--dc23
  [B]
                                                            2012022863

Lucent Books
27500 Drake Rd
Farmington Hills MI 48331

ISBN-13: 978-1-4205-0754-6
ISBN-10: 1-4205-0754-0

Printed in the United States of America
1 2 3 4 5 6 7 16 15 14 13 12

Contents

ame and celebrity are alluring. People are drawn to those who walk in fame's spotlight, whether they are known for great accomplishments or for notorious deeds. The lives of the famous pique public interest and attract attention, perhaps because their experiences seem in some ways so different from, yet in other ways so similar to, our own.

Newspapers, magazines, and television regularly capitalize on this fascination with celebrity by running profiles of famous people. For example, television programs such as *Entertainment Tonight* devote all their programming to stories about entertainment and entertainers. Magazines such as *People* fill their pages with stories of the private lives of famous people. Even newspapers, newsmagazines, and television news frequently delve into the lives of well-known personalities. Despite the number of articles and programs, few provide more than a superficial glimpse at their subjects.

Lucent's People in the News series offers young readers a deeper look into the lives of today's newsmakers, the influences that have shaped them, and the impact they have had in their fields of endeavor and on other people's lives. The subjects of the series hail from many disciplines and walks of life. They include authors, musicians, athletes, political leaders, entertainers, entrepreneurs, and others who have made a mark on modern life and who, in many cases, will continue to do so for years to come.

These biographies are more than factual chronicles. Each book emphasizes the contributions, accomplishments, or deeds that have brought fame or notoriety to the individual and shows how that person has influenced modern life. Authors portray their subjects in a realistic, unsentimental light. For example, Bill Gates—cofounder of the software giant Microsoft—has been instrumental in making personal computers the most vital tool of the modern age. Few dispute his business savvy, his perseverance, or his technical expertise, yet critics say he is ruthless in his dealings with competitors and driven more by his desire to maintain Microsoft's dominance in the computer industry than by an interest in furthering technology.

In these books, young readers will encounter inspiring stories about real people who achieved success despite enormous obstacles. Oprah Winfrey—one of the most powerful, most watched, and wealthiest women in television history—spent the first six years of her life in the care of her grandparents while her unwed mother sought work and a better life elsewhere. Her adolescence was colored by pregnancy at age fourteen, rape, and sexual abuse.

Each author documents and supports his or her work with an array of primary and secondary source quotations taken from diaries, letters, speeches, and interviews. All quotes are footnoted to show readers exactly how and where biographers derive their information and provide guidance for further research. The quotations enliven the text by giving readers eyewitness views of the life and accomplishments of each person covered in the People in the News series.

In addition, each book in the series includes photographs, annotated bibliographies, timelines, and comprehensive indexes. For both the casual reader and the student researcher, the People in the News series offers insight into the lives of today's newsmakers—people who shape the way we live, work, and play in the modern age.

Hollywood's Renaissance Man

James Franco has no typical day. He might be found acting on the set of a major Hollywood movie or sitting in a class in New Haven, Connecticut, or Providence, Rhode Island, learning about literature, modern queer theory, or digital filmmaking. He could be painting or premiering one of his independent films at a film festival. He could be at work on his soon-to-be-published book or in front of a class of students at New York University. Though primarily a celebrity known for his acting work on big-budget action-adventures, comedies, and dramas, Franco is simultaneously pursuing no less than six careers, truly earning him the title of Hollywood's Renaissance Man.

Hollywood's Hardest Worker

Franco first got attention playing in the ensemble cast of the cult-hit television show *Freaks and Geeks* and next achieved celebrity through roles such as James Dean in the made-for-television biopic and as Peter Parker's best friend in the wildly successful *Spider-Man* franchise. Most actors would be thrilled to land these kinds of high-profile projects that come with a hefty paycheck. Yet Franco found himself in the unusual position of not enjoying his status as an A-list actor. Looking around for something more brought him back to college, where he found deep satisfaction and inspiration.

James Franco pursues acting, learning, filmmaking, writing, photography, and other artistic ventures with great enthusiasm.

Franco loved school, and so took more classes—at more schools. In fact, at one point he was enrolled simultaneously in four graduate programs, and then a doctoral program. Most celebrities make news for their relationships, fashion choices, or their pet political or philanthropic causes. Franco, however, is unique for making headlines for not just going back to school, but for enrolling in multiple programs at once. On top of that, he is newsworthy for seeking multiple careers. In addition to actor and student, Franco seeks to become a director (a common move for experienced actors), an independent filmmaker, a writer, a photographer, and a conceptual artist.

The Best at Doing the Most

Hollywood has seen Renaissance men and women before, actors whose interests and abilities in music, writing, or artistic endeavors reveal them to be multitalented. While Franco is clearly multitalented, he is also unique because much of his output is primarily the work of a highly impassioned, diligent, sometimes obsessively workaholic individual, rather than an artistic genius. He has not had easy success in his artistic endeavors, and he has struggled for the modest success he has found. "That struggle is fascinating and a big part of Franco's appeal," explains *New York* magazine reporter Sam Anderson. "He's not a savant or an obvious genius—he's someone of mortal abilities who seems to be working immortally hard."[1]

Interestingly, Franco is not the best at any of the crafts he pursues, but rather the best at pursuing the most crafts. For example, at one point he was pursuing no less than four graduate degree programs in four different states, publishing his debut book, directing and starring in an independent film, and starring in a major movie. None of these efforts was executed flawlessly or critically acclaimed: His real feat was doing them all simultaneously. "Franco grades well on a curve," says Anderson. "He's an excellent writer, for an actor. He's brilliant, for a heartthrob. But he has yet to produce art that's good enough to break the huge gravitational pull of his fame and fly off on its own merits."[2]

The Freedom to Be Happy and Passionate

Franco loves working immortally hard, even if his work is not the best in any one field. It seems as if he has nothing to lose as he ventures into each new project.

In part, this is due to money. Some of the fields that Franco has entered—the world of contemporary art and publishing, for example—are notoriously brutal for newcomers. It is not only difficult for people to get started in these fields, but also for them to make a living from their craft alone. The money Franco has earned from movies, however, has given him the freedom to embark on other artistic ventures without needing to worry whether they become self-sustaining or lucrative. He is perfectly happy to use his Hollywood money to subsidize his other passions.

This makes Franco's confidence for each new project unique. Because he is a movie star, he need not profit from his work, nor does he need to build a reputation in any other field. With nothing riding on the outcomes of his projects, he is free to be purely excited and passionate, an attitude that is obvious to onlookers. As Anderson observes, "No matter how long you stand at the opposite corner of James Franco's art opening, no matter how far from him you stand, no matter how thick the crowd gets, it is impossible not to see that he's prepared, that he's happy, that he likes the argument, the provocation of it all."[3]

Franco is rarely worried that his projects will be panned, or criticized, by the reviews that are sure to follow. He does not ferociously pursue all of his interests in order to win praise. "I am pursuing these things not to like necessarily master them," he once explained. "I'm pursuing [my interests] in what I think is a very humble way."[4] Nonetheless, news and criticism of Franco still lights up the blogosphere and occasionally even appears in major newspapers, as did the 2011 controversy over whether a New York University professor had been fired for giving Franco a D, the time Franco became involved in the Museum of Non-visible Art, or when he enrolled in a PhD program while still finishing several master's degrees. Many times the complaint is that Franco is trying too many things or moving in too many directions at once. Franco does not feel beholden to such a standard. "I never said I was going to go out and be the best director or the best writer or anything," he says. "I just want to do these things because there are certain subjects that I want to tell in a different way."[5]

For Franco this is exactly what makes him happy. With nothing holding him back, America can expect him to continue climbing the ranks of Hollywood's hottest young actors, while simultaneously holding court as a modern Renaissance man.

Chapter 1

Breaking Expectations

James Edward Franco was born on April 19, 1978, to parents Betsy and Doug Franco. From his earliest days, James was an exceptional young person—just not always in the ways that his parents hoped for or expected.

Two Painters Meet

Doug Franco and Betsy Verne met while students at Stanford University, located near Palo Alto in Northern California. Betsy came to Stanford from Cleveland, Ohio, and Doug had grown up in Illinois. Stanford is a prestigious private university renowned for research in a number of fields, including mathematics, sciences, and computer sciences. Doug and Betsy met in drawing classes while at the school. Both were painters, and they connected over their shared interest. While Betsy focused on art and majored in painting, Doug chose something more practical. He majored in mathematics and then earned a master's degree in business administration at Harvard Business School.

Once married, the couple made their home in Palo Alto, California. They had three sons in seven years. James was their firstborn, followed by brothers Thomas and David. All the brothers went by nicknames. Thomas and David were known as Tom and Davy; James went by Ted or Teddy, a nickname for his middle name, Edward. James remembers, "Everyone called me Teddy Bear. When I got older, it was like, 'Enough!'"[6]

James's father held finance and sales management positions at the companies IBM, HP, and Xerox. He was also a Silicon Valley entrepreneur, founding a company called Secure Box, which developed devices to monitor security on shipping containers. Betsy tried several professions when her children were young because it was tough to make a living selling her oil paintings. For a while she answered customer complaints for the phone company. She was also an elementary school teacher. However, caring for her three boys and working left her little time for her art. "With three very adorable, rambunctious young sons in the house, I couldn't even set up my paints," she remembers. "I knew that I needed to find something creative to do, or I would wither."[7]

She began working for an educational publisher as a typist and worked her way up to writing content as an assistant editor. By chance, she was asked to write a few poems for a math textbook. Though she had never written poetry, she channeled her unused artistic energy and dove headfirst into writing for children and young adults. She began writing, illustrating, and publishing children's poetry, mathematics books, and fiction books.

Artistic and Academic

The Franco household was both artistic and academic. In addition to his parents having interest and talent in art, many of James's extended family was artistic, too. Betsy's family ran a prominent art gallery in Cleveland that focused on Japanese art. Her mother and brother became experts on Japanese prints and paintings and frequently traveled to Japan to meet with artists and secure more pieces for their gallery. In addition, Doug Franco's mother was a writer and published a few children's books during her life.

Growing up around so many family members with interest in the arts clearly influenced all of the Franco brothers, who each took an interest in different art forms. From an early age James enjoyed painting. By high school he was taking at least twenty

James Franco with his grandmother Mitzie Verne, a Cleveland art dealer specializing in Japanese art. James Franco's immediate and distant family are very active in both the arts and academics, and James was encouraged in both areas.

hours of art and painting classes a week outside of the normal school day at nearby Stanford. Later in high school, he earned a spot at the California State Summer School for the Arts, a prestigious summer program. Dave Franco, the youngest brother, reflected, "I guess you could say that we have a very strange, artsy family."[8]

With two well-educated parents, learning and achievement were always of utmost importance in the Franco household as

Artistic Brothers

All of the Franco brothers went into artistic fields as adults. Tom, James Franco's middle brother, became a sculptor and illustrator. Tom collaborated with his mother in 2009 to illustrate her young adult novel, *Metamorphosis*. The novel is styled as a notebook in which main character Ovid scribbles stories, notes, and drawings about his classmates' lives as if they were mythological characters.

Both of James Franco's brothers also pursue art as adults. His brother Dave starred in the 2011 film "Fright Night."

Dave Franco, James's youngest brother, is also an actor. He has had a number of guest spots on television shows and small parts in movies. He also played character Cole Aaronson on the television show *Scrubs* during the 2009–2010 season. Dave and his famous brother lived together for a while in Los Angeles and frequently collaborate on projects.

well. Young James met these expectations early and was seemingly driven and industrious from the start. His mother remembers that in kindergarten, James was not content to build simple block towers: He would build towers using every single block in the room. He would also organize all of his toys before he slept. When a friend of the family passed away and death was explained to four-year-old James, he burst into tears, saying, "But I don't want to die! I have so much to do!"[9]

As the boys got older, their parents expected they would do well in school and be well-rounded students. James easily earned good grades and showed a special talent in mathematics, which pleased his father. In fact, James remembers his father pushing him to devote more and more time to math. At one point his father was unhappy to learn how much after-school time he was devoting to the arts. In large part due to his father's urging, James won a prestigious internship at Lockheed Martin, an advanced technology company famous for its aeronautics and satellite divisions.

Life of Crime

When James was in middle and high school, however, he rebelled against his parents' high expectations. He got into trouble from various illegal pursuits. James recalls, "My life of crime started by stealing cologne. That's very true."[10] James and his friends would swipe perfume bottles from department stores like Macy's and then sell them from their gym lockers to make extra cash. James also painted graffiti. He drank with his friends, though he was underage, and even crashed a few cars.

Because of this rebellious behavior, James was arrested for several petty crimes while he was in high school. The arrests added up. James got to the point that if he had been caught doing one more illegal thing, even jaywalking, the court would have sent him to juvenile hall, which is a detention center for delinquent teenagers.

James had to appear before a judge in court because of the arrests. In reviewing his arrests and high school transcripts, the judge noticed a strange discrepancy—James was getting good grades and was involved in impressive extracurricular activities, yet at the same time he was becoming more and more troublesome. The judge was interested to see that he had been accepted to the California State Summer School for the Arts for the following summer and that James got good grades. That judge decided to give him one more chance to turn things around by putting him on probation.

To avoid getting into further trouble, James began spending a lot of time at home. Much of that time was spent reading. James's dad gave him a copy of *As I Lay Dying* by William Faulkner. This

Novelist and screenwriter William Faulkner. In an effort to keep him out of trouble, Franco's father gave him a copy of Faulkner's As I Lay Dying, *which made a big impression on the young man.*

classic novel, which features an experimental blend of stream-of-consciousness writing and multiple narrators, made a lasting impression. "Essentially, the book is a bunch of smaller, linked episodes," said James. "I really love the interior lives of the characters and the multiple perspectives—they have inspired my own stories."[11] James fell in love with Faulkner from this book.

The threat of juvenile detention, the judge's gift of one more chance, and the time he spent alone reflecting motivated James to turn things around. He realized that the reason he spent so much time getting into trouble was because he was pushing against his parents' expectations while trying to figure out where he fit in at school. "It was teen angst." he said years later. "I was uncomfortable in my own skin. I was shy. I changed my ways just in time to get good grades."[12] James refocused on his schoolwork, earned exceptionally high SAT scores, and began to put more energy into pursuing arts and literature, though his dad continued to push him to focus on mathematics.

Secret

One of the reasons James felt uncomfortable was because he was a naturally shy kid who did not know exactly where he fit in. Before entering high school he dabbled in a number of sports, including soccer, baseball, and basketball, but was never the best on the team. He did not have many friends and did not have a clear niche. Looking back, he often calls himself a loner.

Another thing that set him apart from his peers was that throughout high school, James nursed a secret dream to be an actor. "I know this (that I wanted to be an actor) because I had pictures of actors all over my walls at a very young age. River Phoenix, Johnny Depp," he says. "I wanted to act, but I was scared."[13] James was scared partly because he had never known anyone who was an actor. His family was full of artists and writers, but no actors. Also, living in suburban Palo Alto, he was too far from major acting hubs like Los Angeles or New York to make a career in acting seem possible.

During his junior and senior years in high school, however, he dated a girl named Jasmine who was involved in drama. She performed in school plays and applied to acting school while the two dated. James accompanied Jasmine on one of her auditions. As he waited for her in the hall outside her audition, he overheard some people rehearsing. James thought he could do at least as well as them. "I just thought, like, I mean they weren't the worst

In high school Franco began to realize that he really wanted to be an actor, like River Phoenix, who starred in the 1991 film My Own Private Idaho with Keanu Reeves.

in the world (but) I think I could probably do that,"[14] he recalls. James realized acting was not something he should fear. Shortly after this realization, he learned he had a friend who was doing commercials in San Francisco. This friend told James how easy filming commercials was—that it just involved saying a few lines, bouncing a basketball, or reenacting normal snippets of other everyday activities.

Jealousy was the final experience that helped get James onto a stage. Around this time, a male student who was in the drama program with Jasmine wrote a romantic one-act play for two actors. The student asked Jasmine to play the female part—but it involved kissing. James was upset and begged her not to do it. Jasmine, however, was a dedicated actress, so refused to turn the part down.

Frustrated, James used the situation as an excuse to enroll in drama classes his senior year. There were two plays running that year, and James auditioned for both. He turned out to be a natural: He was cast in the lead the very first time he tried out. Both plays were dark and heavy. One was about a man who goes crazy and eventually murders his wife. For James, being onstage was eye-opening. "That was great," he said. "I discovered that you can just get everything out when you're acting!"[15] Acting in these plays helped James begin to imagine himself acting outside of school, in a more professional setting.

College

James had originally been interested in going to college to study art. With a stint at the California State Summer School for the Arts and a developed talent in painting, he thought art school was the perfect place to explore his burgeoning interest in art and acting. His parents, however, were not supportive. "My parents weren't big on that idea," James remembers. "They didn't want to pay for it. I actually really wanted to go to RISD [the Rhode

Despite his desire to be an actor, Franco's parents wanted him to get an education, so he enrolled in the University of California at Los Angeles.

Island School of Design], but they didn't even let me apply. They said they wouldn't pay for it."[16] His father especially expected James to go to a regular university and train for a career in a practical field.

James and his parents struck a compromise. He applied and was accepted to the University of California–Los Angeles (UCLA); but rather than major in math, as his father wanted, James was to major in English. James had cultivated a strong interest in literature in high school. With Faulkner as his hero, he felt that the English Department was the right place for him to be if he were going to attend a conventional college.

Once in Los Angeles, over half the people James met were involved in the film industry. All around him people were trying to make it as actors. Though he had enrolled in college, he still held tight to his dream of being an actor. UCLA has an excellent drama program, and James attempted to switch into the program during his first year. But because he had not auditioned for the program before beginning his freshman year, school policy was such that he would have to wait two years, until his junior (third) year, to try out.

Two years felt like a lifetime to the impatient nineteen-year-old. Rather than wait, he dropped out of college after only one year. "All my friends looked at me with pity thinking I made a pretty poor move," he said. "But after you take the leap, you know in your heart if you made the right move or not."[17]

"Pay Me What You Can"

James's parents were upset by his decision to drop out of UCLA in order to pursue acting full-time. "You're being an idiot,"[18] was how his father put it. His parents had paid his tuition and supported him while he was in school, but they were unwilling to do so once he dropped out. So James had to support himself. He looked around everywhere for a job but had trouble finding one. Finally, a friend suggested, "Are you too good to work at McDonald's?"[19] James replied, "I guess not. I'm doing this because it's what I really want to do, so I'll work at McDonald's, if that's what it takes."[20]

Franco did not enjoy school and he soon dropped out to pursue acting. In the meantime, he got a job at McDonald's to pay the bills.

From McDonald's to Pizza Hut

After working at a McDonald's restaurant for about three months, James Franco got his first paid acting gig: a Pizza Hut commercial. The commercial featured a computer-generated Elvis Presley, and Franco was a member of a group of guys hanging out outside the restaurant. Franco recounted the plot of the commercial for the website the Days of Yore, which interviews artists about their pre-fame years: "We were, like, in this dirt parking lot, a gang of dudes. The main guy was like, 'Have you heard the news?!' And we were like, 'What?!' 'Elvis is in Pizza Hut and he's eating a deep dish pizza!' And we were like, 'No way! *Deep dish*?!' Then it cuts to the Pizza Hut where the computer generated Elvis is eating the pizza and he's, like, singing."

Franco admits it was not his finest acting moment, but it was his first paid acting job, and he never had to work a side job again.

Quoted in Astri von Arbin Ahlander. "James Franco." Days of Yore. www.thedaysofyore.com/james-franco.

James was hired and spent most of his shifts working as a cashier at the drive-through window. "They didn't put me anywhere near the burgers," he remembers. "Then, when I had to do the food window, I just got too confused and everything got backed up."[21] The job did not pay much, but James shared an apartment with friends and slept on their couch, so it was enough to support himself while he took acting classes. James also used the job as an opportunity to practice his acting skills on the girls who drove through. "I was just getting into acting, so I'd practice different accents on the girls. I'd be French and then Italian. One girl who liked me came around the drive-through again and said,

'Could you give me some Italian lessons?' I don't know what she was thinking because I was doing an awful Italian accent."[22]

James enrolled in acting classes at Playhouse West, a repertory theater in Los Angeles. There he studied under famous acting teachers such as Jeff Goldblum and Robert Carnegie, who became a mentor to James. Carnegie was impressed by James's dedication and saw that he was pulling double duty, trying to both earn a living himself and hone his craft. James poignantly remembers Carnegie telling him, "Pay me what you can and down the road, you can pay me back."[23] James was touched and motivated to find a mentor who believed in him. He threw himself into acting classes, immersing himself in his dream. With dedication James found acting work in Hollywood, enabling him to pay Carnegie back for the loan within just a few years. Though acting was not the path his parents expected or wanted for him, James knew in his heart that he was doing the right thing.

Chapter 2

Disappearing Franco

After fifteen months of acting training at Playhouse West, James Franco had honed an extreme form of method acting. In Hollywood, Franco became known for the obsessive way he researched and prepared in order to disappear into the roles he played. As he climbed Hollywood's career ladder, however, Franco began to find that this process of acting was not always satisfying—something that caused him to question his commitment to his singular goal of being an actor.

"Too Much Flavor"

In 1997 Franco began auditioning for roles in Los Angeles. He tried out for a variety of parts, landing small roles in commercials and guest spots on established television shows. Franco was incredibly dedicated and serious about every audition that came his way. He would research the smallest of roles and envision an entire world for each character he played, no matter how small. "When I was starting out, doing guest spots on TV, and even commercials, I would go in with a whole crazy wardrobe and some terrible accent," he remembers. "Obviously I was doing too much. If you bring too much flavor, it's absurd."[24]

In 1999, after about a year and a half of television guest spots and commercials, James Franco won a role in the pilot (first episode) of a new comedy-drama television show called *Freaks and Geeks*.

James Franco, second from left, poses with the cast of the 1999 television show Freaks and Geeks. Though only twelve episodes aired, the show had a strong following, and Franco dug deep into his character.

Despite being canceled after just 12 episodes during its 1999-2000 season, the show developed a cult following after the episodes were released on DVD. The show followed two sets of students (a set of "freaks" and a set of "geeks") at a Michigan high school. The school was loosely based on the school that the show's creator, Judd Apatow, had attended in Michigan.

Franco immediately set himself apart from his costars. For example, he took it upon himself to fly to Michigan and spend a week in the high school the show was based on. Everyone on the show—the creators and cast—thought this was over-the-top and unnecessary, but Franco thought it would help him to understand his character better. On set, Franco was committed to method acting, even though he was the only one of the ensemble cast who employed the technique. Franco created a backstory for his

Judd Apatow

Judd Apatow is a comedy producer, director, and screenwriter. He initially wrote for several well-known movies such as *The Cable Guy* (1996) and Adam Sandler's *The Wedding Singer* (1998). After the success of his own show, *Freaks and Geeks*, Apatow produced a string of major hits, including *The 40-Year-Old Virgin* (2005), *Talladega Nights* (2006), *Knocked Up* (2007), and *Superbad* (2007).

Apatow frequently works with the same cast across his many projects and has fostered the careers of a small group of actors, many of whom were initially in *Freaks and Geeks*. Known as the Apatow gang, this group includes Seth Rogen, Evan Goldberg, Jonah Hill, Jason Segel, Jay Baruchel, Martin Starr, Jason Schwartzman, Elizabeth Banks, Paul Rudd, and Apatow's wife, Leslie Mann. The Apatow gang—or Apatown, as they are also known—is famous for churning out hilariously funny, though raunchy, movies that rely on this recurring cast of ensemble actors. In 2008 Franco again appeared in an Apatown production when he and Rogen starred in *Pineapple Express*.

Producer, director, and screenwriter Judd Apatow has worked with James Franco on multiple occasions. In fact, Franco would be considered part of the "Apatow gang."

character, Daniel Desario, which was not written into the scripts. He imagined Desario was possibly abused by his father and that this abuse informed his relationships.

Franco's cast mates, however, were unaware of this backstory, and this was a problem on occasion. During one scene in which

Franco was arguing with Busy Phillips, who played his character's girlfriend, Phillips was supposed to slap Franco lightly on the arm. When she did, Franco shouted, "Don't you ever [expletive] touch me again!" and threw her to the ground, even though the script did not call for the action. "I had the wind knocked out of me,"[25] recalls Phillips, who ran to her trailer crying.

Other habits made Franco a curious cast mate. He was frequently seen with a lot of books under his arm and would spend his downtime reading. Apatow recalls, "In between takes, he would read 'Moby Dick' and no one knew if he was actually reading it or it if was just some sort of showing off."[26] In addition, Franco was the only actor who asked to shadow the show's director and did other behind-the-scenes sort of activities, such as spending a week watching an entire reel of film be cut together into an episode.

Despite his genuine commitment to the process, Franco's behavior led his fellow cast members to suspect he was an overeager show-off just looking to impress. Nonetheless, Franco had comedic talent that Apatow noticed, and his earnest dedication to the show eventually impressed others. Fellow *Freaks and Geeks* alum Seth Rogen wrote scenes for the show. He remembers that Franco wanted to get together to help Rogen write and to read what he had written, an unusual activity for an actor who was not also writer. Rogen says, "I remember at the time thinking it was crazy that he would do that."[27]

James Franco Is James Dean

While starring in *Freaks and Geeks*, Franco continued to audition for other roles. In 2000 he won the starring role in a TV biopic on the legendary actor James Dean. Dean was a popular actor in the early 1950s. He played iconic roles in *Rebel Without a Cause* (1955) and *East of Eden* (1955), but tragically died in a car accident at age twenty-four. The biopic was intended to show the darker side of Dean, who was a talented actor but a troubled soul; the movie showed how his father shunned him and sent him to live with relatives at age nine when his mother died.

In order to fully inhabit the character and authentically replicate some of Dean's loneliness, Franco cut off communication with

Franco immersed himself in the role of James Dean for a television biopic in 2000. He read about, watched, and followed the habits of the old Hollywood actor to better represent him on the screen.

his family and girlfriend for four months. During this period, Franco spent extensive time with two of the men Dean knew in real life—Martin Landau, one of his good friends, and Leonard Rosenman, Dean's roommate and the composer of the scores for two of Dean's movies. Franco also read numerous books and incessantly watched Dean's movies. "It was a very lonely existence," Franco says. "If I wasn't on a set, I was watching James Dean. That was my whole thinking. James Dean. James Dean."[28] In addition, Franco took up Dean's habits and hobbies and began smoking, riding a motorcycle, and playing the guitar and the bongos.

Franco's intense method acting paid off. His portrayal of Dean attracted much praise. The director and executive producer of the movie, Mark Rydell, who also knew Dean in real life, said, "Jimmy Dean was the most dedicated actor that I've ever met—until I met Franco. His achievement is one of the most remarkable things we've seen in years. My God, you feel like he's channeling Jimmy. He found the essence of Jimmy without losing himself."[29] Critics and other actors and directors also took notice. Franco's performance earned him a Golden Globe Award for Best Actor in a TV movie, as well as Emmy and Screen Actors Guild Award nominations.

City by the Sea

Franco's extraordinary work made him an actor to watch, opening the door to lots of auditions for new and different roles. In fact, after seeing *James Dean* (2001), Robert De Niro, an iconic Hollywood actor and director, specifically sought Franco to audition for a role in his upcoming film, *City by the Sea* (2002). Franco was cast in the role of Joey, the homeless, junkie son of a cop, played by De Niro. As he did for the Dean role, Franco went through a complete transformation to play Joey, going to extreme measures to embody the role. To get inside the head of an irresponsible, drug-addicted young man, Franco went to the streets. He went to the Los Angeles downtown mission—a social service organization for the homeless—to meet people who lived similarly to his character. He also tried being homeless himself. He lived by the beach in Santa Monica and Venice, California, as well as on the streets of New York and New Jersey.

Robert De Niro sought out Franco for the role of a homeless junkie in the 2002 film, City by the Sea. Franco spent a lot of time among the homeless and talking to drug addicts to get into this role.

To play a kid who was so desperate, I hung around in Asbury Park, NJ, which is this rundown town. I dressed down, poured beer on myself and really started to stink so I looked like a strung out guy. I took no money with me and many vans drove up and the people inside handed me a meal. That happened in New York, too. I was sitting on a stoop in St. Marks [a church that serves homeless] and some guy came up and he showed me a little stairwell where I could sleep. It was a nice world to look into.[30]

Franco did, however, draw the line at actually taking drugs in order to understand his addicted character. "There's a line I won't cross," he said of his willingness to live his character's lives. "I don't murder people and I don't do drugs."[31] Instead, Franco talked to drug users and addicts to understand what his character was going through. "I needed to know the technical aspects of taking drugs and the effects that the influence of drugs would have on a person. But there's also a specific attitude and lifestyle from that world. A lot of the guys in the treatment centers would help me with that."[32]

Franco's resulting portrayal was convincing. Though the movie was widely criticized by reviewers as trite and predictable, several noted that Franco played his part with authenticity. In addition to getting noticed for his acting, many commented on his good looks. As one critic wrote, "He's a knockout even playing someone who's strung out."[33] Franco continued to audition for new roles; after *City by the Sea* his calendar was full of future projects, including a role in the blockbuster superhero movie *Spider-Man* (2002).

Franco originally auditioned for the lead role in *Spider-Man*, Peter Parker, but was instead cast as Parker's brooding best friend, Harry Osborn. Since Franco was not a comic book fan going into the movie, he read hundreds of *Spider-Man* issues. To get into his role as a wealthy, troublesome kid who had been kicked out of prestigious boarding schools, Franco visited, stayed at, and met with students at several such schools in New England.

Again, his work paid off. The *Spider-Man* movie and its two sequels had blockbuster ticket sales. More than any other role, Franco's portrayal of Harry Osborn and the alter-ego the Green Goblin ushered him into the world of A-list Hollywood movie stars.

Sonny

Franco underwent a similar process of transformation for another move he made in 2002. That year he was cast as the lead in *Sonny*, which marked his transition to big-screen leading man. In this movie, directed by Nicolas Cage, Franco played a male prostitute named Sonny. After returning home from a stint in the army, Sonny's mother—who runs a brothel in New Orleans—tries to get him to rejoin the family business. Sonny, however, is reluctant.

To become this character, Franco undertook another extensive research campaign. He went to New Orleans and interviewed male prostitutes. He also sought out men in this line of work in San Francisco. Cage accompanied Franco on some of his trips and was impressed by Franco's intensity and dedication to the research process, though worried at some points that Franco was putting himself in danger. Franco admitted there were certain times he felt afraid. "When I research a role it does get a little crazy and maybe even a little stupid," he told Cage. But ultimately, Franco believes the risk is worth it if he can dig deeper into a character. "I never want to say, 'I held back here,' or 'I could have done that but didn't,'" he said. "Nothing bad happened to me [researching *Sonny*], but there was one time when a couple of

The 2002 movie, Sonny, starred James Franco in the lead role of a male prostitute. Once again, Franco did much research to prepare for this role, talking to many real-life prostitutes to learn what their lives were like.

guys were going out on a date, and they took me so I could see how it all went down. In the back of my mind I thought, 'If we get busted this will be hard to explain.'"[34]

"I Was Just Obsessed"

Franco's dedication to acting was obvious. In addition to thoroughly, even obsessively, researching his roles, he also continued to take acting classes at Playhouse West. Between films, he did script work at the school with Robert Carnegie, his mentor. He also occasionally performed in plays, without publicity or fanfare. "It puts me in an environment that takes acting seriously," Franco reflected on his continued study at Playhouse West. "It also refocuses me, so I'm not clowning around."[35]

Franco devoted himself so thoroughly to acting that he left himself little time to do anything else. He did not even date. "I put everything into my acting," he explained. "I would sign on to movies eight, nine … months in advance and literally prepare every day for these roles. Because I thought—I was just obsessed. I wanted to be the best actor I could be."[36] Carnegie thought Franco's obsession required a discipline that was remarkable. "The thing that I always try to get across about James when I talk to people is the dedication, the discipline and the hard work that's gone into his success," Carnegie said. "This is a special young actor."[37]

Flying, Boxing, and Sword Fighting

Between 2002 and 2005 Franco filmed a number of movies in rapid succession, playing a wide array of roles. His intense process of getting into character made transforming for these physically demanding roles the most challenging process he had faced yet.

After completing a war movie called *The Great Raid*, released in 2005, Franco signed on to do *Flyboys* (2006), after the director of the movie, Tony Bill, took him flying in his own vintage two-seater plane. *Flyboys* is about young Americans who went to France during World War I to volunteer as fighter pilots before the United States entered the war. They joined the Lafayette Escadrille, a

Rabbit Bandini Productions

In 2003, with the help of his friend Vince Jolivette, James Franco created his own film production company, Rabbit Bandini Productions. Jolivette and Franco met in an acting class in 1996. After working together for a number of years, they wanted to create a production company to support independent filmmakers, including themselves.

Franco directs most of the films released through the production company and usually stars in them. Jolivette often takes minor roles as well. Jolivette manages the day-to-day business of the company, while Franco primarily initiates film ideas, directs, and stars in projects. The first release of Rabbit Bandini Productions was *The Ape* in 2005, a dark comedy about a frustrated writer who finds himself living with a talking, clothes-wearing ape.

The name *Rabbit Bandini* stems from Franco and Jolivette's shared loved of literature. *Rabbit* is from Jolivette's favorite novel, *Rabbit at Rest* by John Updike, and *Bandini* is the last name of the main character in John Fante's novel *Ask the Dust*.

French air squadron, becoming the first American fighter pilots in the war. Franco was cast as the lead and prepared for filming by getting his pilot's license. Franco thought knowing how to fly would make his portrayal of a wartime aviator more authentic. He was inspired by Steve McQueen, a real-life pilot who also played a pilot in the movie *The War Lover* (1962). "You just watch him in and around the plane [in *The War Lover*] and it's so natural and detailed," said Franco. "It's because he was a real pilot."[38]

For his next project, *Annapolis*, Franco added another skill to his résumé: boxing. This 2006 film is set at the U.S. Naval Academy, and Franco plays underdog cadet Jake Huard, who ultimately proves himself in the ring. To prepare, Franco spent eight months learning to box and getting into shape. Physical skills were also a requirement for his next movie, *Tristan + Isolde*

Franco continued to research for his roles. For the 2006 movie Flyboys, in which he played a World War II fighter pilot, Franco learned how to fly a plane.

(2006). Franco learned to wield a broadsword and spent months learning horse-riding tricks.

As Tristan, Franco appeared in several sword-fighting sequences and did stunts such as jumping between horses. Because of his ample preparation, few stunt doubles were used. His commitment also resulted in some on-set injuries, though none terribly serious. The injuries did not deter Franco from his hands-on approach. "I want to make a performance as realistic as possible, unless there's some strange requirement," he explained. "Taking those steps is what gives me the confidence to say, 'Okay, I can play this role,' as well as the confidence to fall on my face."[39]

Franco hoped starring in these action-adventure movies would launch his career upward. Unfortunately, none of the films did well in theaters—the critical response was lukewarm and sometimes negative. "'Annapolis' is less like a movie than a virus—one that clings so tenaciously to its host genre that it begins to take on the characteristics of a real movie, even though it's just faking,"[40] wrote *Salon.com*'s Stephanie Zacharek. *Flyboys*, meanwhile, was an outright bomb. As one critic put it, "Just about everything in the video-gamey World War I picture 'Flyboys' rings false, although the planes certainly are terrific."[41]

Seeing movies flop that he had poured so much energy into was upsetting to Franco. In addition, he began to resent that so much of his research went unused in big-budget action movies, which typically focus more on special effects and fight sequences than on character development. He began to question the value of his intense preparation process. "You can learn all you want about a character," he realized, "but … at a certain point the research becomes excess … about 70 percent of [my] research would just go unused. It would never be seen in the movie. And that was very frustrating to me."[42]

Furthermore, Franco, like many other movie stars, was encouraged to sign up for movie projects that did not necessarily interest him but were good for his career. He began to deeply resent working this way. "I did these movies that I just plainly shouldn't have done," he reflected. "But they were movies that I would put in the category of things people said well this would be good for your career. But not necessarily things that I would say to myself well, this is the movie I've always wanted to do."[43] Friend and fellow actor Seth Rogen thinks movie studios saw for Franco something different than the actor wanted for himself. "I think the agencies saw, 'Ooh, we've got a young handsome actor dude. Let's put him in a bunch of action movies and he'll be Tom Cruise in 10 years,'" said Rogen. "That was what people were going for. I think he was pressed into it."[44]

"An Eye Opener"

In 2006 Franco realized he was on the wrong path. "[The failure of the movies] was a great thing. It was an eye opener," he explained. "And I said … I can't do this anymore. … I really couldn't continue acting in that way. I couldn't continue acting if it was going to be like that, doing movies where I didn't enjoy the process. And I didn't like the results."[45] Taking stock, Franco sought to express himself in other ways. He began to envy the fact that directors had control over a movie's story and could determine a vision for a project. He also began thinking about the English degree he had left behind nearly ten years ago. Ready to explore other avenues, in a dramatic move for an already famous actor, Franco reenrolled at UCLA.

Chapter 3

The Actor Goes Back to School

After nine years of acting, James Franco found himself wanting something else. He had climbed the Hollywood ladder to become a leading man, only to realize he did not want acting to be his whole life. Franco therefore decided to return to UCLA, the school he dropped out of ten years earlier.

UCLA

While Franco contemplated a career shift, he took extension classes at UCLA, classes meant to serve as continuing education for working adults, seniors, or others who need a less traditional class structure. Franco took a class in literature and one in creative writing. He found them exciting and satisfying, leading him to reenroll in the university full-time to finish the bachelor's degree he had begun right out of high school.

When Franco returned to UCLA in 2006, he approached his education with the same intensity as he had his acting career. He wanted to take more classes each quarter than the typical student does, so he petitioned the student advising office to allow him to take more credits than the limit, which is nineteen per quarter, or 3-4 typical classes. As he put it, "I wasn't going back to school just to get by with a little amount of work."[46] However, it took Franco a couple of weeks to persuade Penny Hein-Unruh, assistant vice provost of academic advising, that he was able to handle the additional workload. Ultimately, Hein-Unruh was won over by Franco's commitment; she granted his requests. Hein-Unruh recalls, "[Franco's] was truly just a thirst for knowledge, a sense that 'I've waited this long, I'm going to take advantage of everything.'"[47] Each quarter, Franco's course load ranged from twenty to sixty-two credits.

Though he majored in writing and literature, the spread of Franco's classes often reflected his diverse academic interests. Franco studied the philosophy of science, French, and American Holocaust literature, in addition to the numerous traditional literature and creative writing classes he took. Though he was an English major, Franco took a senior seminar—a high-level class designed for majors in the field—in political theology. His professor, Ken Reinhard, remembers the intensity with which Franco approached the objects of his curiosity. "He wanted to know all about these very, very recent, hot theorists, people like Slavoj Zizek and Alain Badiou."[48]

Franco also worked closely with Janel Munguia, the English Department faculty adviser, during his time at UCLA. Munguia helped him stay on track with his major requirements and find opportunities in the English Department. For example, Munguia convinced Franco to submit his poetry from class to poetry contests. He won honorable mention for a piece he submitted to the May Merrill Miller Poetry Awards. Munguia also encouraged Franco to write an honors thesis novel and helped arrange for him to work with Mona Simpson, a successful novelist and UCLA English professor.

The Student Goes Back to Work

Ironically, just as Franco fully immersed himself in school, new acting roles began to find him. In 2005, Franco flew to Texas to attend the Austin Film Festival where his independent film, "The Ape," was showing. Through a chance encounter at the Austin airport, Franco ran into Judd Apatow, who was also in town for the same festival. Apatow mentioned that he and Seth Rogen were collaborating on a film, and he invited Franco to read for one of the starring roles. The result was Franco's spin as Saul in the *Pineapple Express*, an action-comedy following the adventures of two pot smokers. The movie was popular and showcased Franco's

Franco returned to school with a newfound desire to learn, but he continued to take acting roles, such as in the 2008 Judd Apatow comedy Pineapple Express. *Franco, center, starred with Seth Rogan, left, and Danny McBride. Franco received critical praise for this comedic turn.*

comic talent, something none of his projects had since *Freaks* and *Geeks*. Michael Phillips, a reviewer for the *Chicago Tribune*, called Franco "blissfully funny,"[49] while reviewers for *Slant* described his performance as "pitch-perfect."[50]

While working on his degree, Franco also filmed *Spider-Man 3* (2007) and secured a role in *Milk* (2008), about San Francisco's first openly gay elected official, Harvey Milk. Franco played Milk's boyfriend, Scott Smith. *Milk* filmed entirely in San Francisco, requiring Franco to spend a lot of time flying back and forth between there and Los Angeles.

Filming three movies while also attending college full-time was no easy task, and Franco was often pulled in different directions. He had to miss classes during filming, but he worked hard to stay connected. He asked friends in each of his classes to record the lectures, and he listened to them at night in his trailer on the movie set. Franco also spent a lot of time on set doing homework and reading. Though he always had the habit of carrying books around on set, now as a college student he read even more furiously. "We used to laugh because in between takes he'd be reading *The Iliad* on set," remembered Apatow. "With him, it was always James Joyce or something."[51]

Franco's roles in *Pineapple Express* and *Milk* satisfied him in a way other projects had not. He enjoyed the process of filming both and especially liked working with Apatow and Rogen on *Pineapple Express* and with director Gus Van Sant and Sean Penn in *Milk*. In addition, *Milk* received much critical praise, giving him a movie on his résumé of which he was proud. As movie critic Kenneth Turan said, "This film wants us to understand both how far we've come as a society and that it is still not far enough."[52]

The success of these films combined with the box office explosion of *Spider-Man 3* (2007) catapulted Franco's career at a time when he had chosen to step back from acting. Franco, however, was clear that school was exactly where we wanted to be. He said:

Some people would say [going to school instead of acting is] really stupid. It's not like I'm gonna stop acting. It's just that before I did these two movies [*Pineapple Express* and *Milk*], I was really tired of acting.

I was putting a ton of work in and not getting as much satisfaction out of it. So I just needed something else to focus my attention on, to take the pressure off. Turns out that I love school.[53]

Graduate School

Franco earned his bachelor's degree and graduated from UCLA in June 2008. He maintained an impressive grade point average of 3.5 even while he acted in movies and took an overload of classes. The experience left him wanting more, so he next applied to four graduate programs to continue his studies, three in New York and one in North Carolina. Upon being admitted to all four, he decided there was no reason he could not go to all of them.

Therefore, in the fall of 2008, Franco moved to New York City, where he enrolled in Columbia University's master of fine arts (MFA) in creative writing program; New York University's (NYU's) Tisch School of the Arts' filmmaking program; and Brooklyn

There were so many subjects that interested Franco that he enrolled in four graduate programs at four different schools at the same time. He continued to work classroom lectures around his acting commitments.

College's MFA in creative writing program. Franco also enrolled in the Warren Wilson College for an MFA in poetry. Warren Wilson is in North Carolina and runs its MFA classes entirely during ten-day residency periods that take place in January and July. Franco commuted there by plane for these sessions.

For Franco, enrolling in four graduate programs simultaneously made an odd kind of sense. "You know, I've always been interested in art, literature, film and acting," he said. "I thought why not just pursue them all seriously, see ... if they can all come together and how."[54] However, nearly everyone around him doubted Franco could undertake all these things, especially all at once. Graduate admissions officers would have been concerned if Franco had only been attempting to enroll full-time in one program while maintaining a Hollywood acting career; that he was enrolling in four required much explanation.

John Tintori, the chair of NYU's filmmaking program, remembers he had to be convinced of Franco's sincerity during his entrance interview, a part of the application process. "[Franco] was an hour early. He just sat outside my office waiting. In the interview, the two faculty members who were with me were skeptical and really held his feet to the fire. He said, 'I am not going to be the guy who's not pulling his weight.'"[55] Once the semester and program got underfoot, Tintori confirmed that Franco was indeed pulling his weight. "He's loading up and doing extra credit," Tintori confirmed. "Normally, we're a three-year program. My guess is he'll probably finish in two and a half years. A few months ago, [Franco] said, 'I really like it here. Is it okay, after I finish all my requirements—can I keep taking classes?'"[56]

Franco was certainly interested in taking classes, and not just at NYU. After he finished the Columbia MFA writing program in two years, graduating in June 2010 he embarked on a PhD in English at Yale University. Franco enrolled full-time at Yale even while he continued to take classes at and work toward degrees at NYU, Brooklyn College, and Warren Wilson. Not one to limit himself, the same semester he began commuting to Yale in New Haven, Connecticut (about two hours north of New York City), he also began taking classes at the Rhode Island School of Design (RISD) in Providence, Rhode Island, which is an hour from New

Haven and three hours from New York City. Like Yale, RISD is one of the most prestigious schools of its kind in the country. Interestingly, an eighteen-year-old Franco had wanted to apply to RISD, but his parents would not let him. Fifteen years later, there Franco was in the digital and media department, working toward yet another MFA degree.

Academic Lightweight?

While in each of these programs, Franco also continued to act in major movies, on a popular daytime soap opera, and in his own independent film projects. Though many of the latter started as class assignments, Franco went on to develop the films further, honing his skills as a director, and then sent several of the films out to be screened on the independent film festival circuit. He also published some of his short stories during the same time period.

Overambitious?

Though James Franco is a dedicated student, at times he is overambitious and commits to events he ultimately cannot follow through with or starts projects he cannot or will not finish. For example, Franco was invited to be the commencement speaker at UCLA in 2009, the year after he graduated. He initially agreed, and the university announced the exciting news. Just days before the ceremony, though, Franco reported he would not be able to honor the commitment due to conflicts with his next film.

Another time, at Yale, Franco made plans to produce and direct a student musical. The script was written, auditions were held, and roles cast. In the end, however, Franco had to pull out of the project. Since the musical was entirely structured around him—it was called *James Franco Presents*—the production collapsed entirely and did not see the stage.

The head of New York University's directing department, Jay Anania, appears at the Tribeca Film Festival. NYU professor José Angel Santana alleged that the university gave James Franco a pass as a student, despite his lax performance, because Franco hired Anania to write and direct one of his films.

That Franco could balance all these projects with his graduate programs impressed some, yet made many others skeptical that he was actually actively working on all that he said he was. Bloggers and opinion journalists pounced when a photo was posted online of Franco sleeping in what appeared to be a Columbia lecture hall. Many took the photo as evidence that Franco was slacking off, an academic lightweight who was skating by on his fame.

Even more controversial was a claim by professor José Angel Santana that he had been fired from NYU in 2010 because he gave Franco a D for missing twelve out of fourteen classes of his Directing the Actor II course. In a lawsuit Santana filed against NYU in Manhattan's Supreme Court, Santana suggested Franco's attendance and performance were similarly poor in his other NYU classes. Santana said professors put up with him and gave him good grades because Franco had hired the head of NYU's directing department, Jay Anania, to write and direct one of his independent films. "The school has bent over backwards to create a Franco-friendly environment, that's for sure," said Santana. "They've turned the NYU graduate film degree into swag for James Franco's purposes, a possession, something you can buy."[57]

"The Opposite of ADHD"

NYU, however, dismissed Santana's allegation and rejected claims that one of its professors would use a student to gain publicity. Franco never responded to Santana's claims but was defended by professors and peers who painted a very different picture of him as a student. John Williams, one of Franco's professors as well as his advisor at Yale, described Franco as a dedicated student. "I've been James' professor, and it struck me as highly uncharacteristic for him to just 'blow off class,' as several articles are suggesting,"[58] said Williams.

Even while Franco was filming a Disney adaption of the Wizard of Oz in Detroit, he managed to make it to all but one of Williams's classes. Furthermore, he often showed up having read far more than was required and came prepared with pages and pages of his own written reflections. Once Williams realized the amount of time Franco was afforded on movie sets to read and study, and the fact that he can afford a personal assistant to take care of chores and errands, he said, "The thing I found myself wondering was not 'How does James do it?' but rather 'Why aren't more Hollywood actors earning Ph.Ds?'"[59]

Interviewer Sam Anderson also confirmed that Franco in fact does all the things he says he does. He followed the actor while doing a story on him and interviewed Franco and people around him. "When I asked people if Franco actually does all of his own homework," said Anderson, "some of them literally laughed right out loud at me, because apparently homework is all James Franco ever really wants to do."[60] After months of meeting Franco for interviews, following him to classes, visiting his art exhibits, and watching him work, Anderson concluded:

> [Franco] seems to suffer, or to benefit, from the opposite of ADHD: a superhuman ability to focus that allows him to shuttle quickly between projects and to read happily in the midst of chaos. He hates wasting time—a category that includes, for him, sleeping. ... He's engineered life so he can spend all this time either making or learning about art.[61]

Several of Franco's professors have not only been impressed with his dedication as a student, but also pleased that Franco leaves his Hollywood persona behind once in class. "He's very good at not attracting attention to himself and blending in," says Michael Warner, chair of Yale's English Department and another of Franco's professors. "He looks with thoughtful attention at the people around him and doesn't display Hollywood wattage."[62]

No Sleep

Though Franco may attempt to blend in on his many campuses, he is hardly a normal student. He is a compulsive coffee drinker, a regular at campus coffee shops and bookstores with cafés. He particularly likes one in the Yale area, and though he goes there to sit quietly and study, he is rarely left alone. Other students, mostly women, often introduce themselves. At Yale, student journalists chronicle his every move on campus, and student Twitter accounts report sightings of him in the city. Some students have taken to wearing James Franco masks around New Haven. Sometimes Franco likes to keep a low profile; other times he prefers to indulge his fans. In March 2011, for example, he posted photos online from inside his room at the Study at Yale, the boutique hotel he stays in when he does not return to his New York City apartment after classes.

Franco uses his celebrity in positive ways that help his class assignments and extracurricular projects achieve a grander scale than the typical student. For example, for student film assignments, he is able to hire professional camera operators. He has the resources to develop short class assignments into full-length film projects. Rather than limiting their display to campus, Franco can show them at professional, independent film festivals, as he did with the documentary he made in 2008, *Saturday Night*. When Franco was taking an individualized study course on film theory, the other student and the professor flew to the set of the big-budget movie Franco was filming at the time to see theory in action.

Franco's schedule has him constantly moving from class lecture hall to film location, award ceremony to art opening or interview. He sleeps only a little at a time, focused on doing as much as possible with his time.

The *Yale Daily News*

The *Yale Daily News* (*YDN*), the student newspaper of Yale University, maintains a student culture blog where student journalists can publish short articles. During his time as a student, James Franco was a recurring topic of the blog and the focus of many articles in the newspaper, not all of them positive.

One particularly public exchange occurred after Franco hosted the Academy Awards in early 2011 and tweeted photos from backstage. Cokey Cohen, a *YDN* journalist, wrote a quickly worded 3:00 A.M. blog post criticizing Franco's tweets. Franco fired back a photo of himself with an expletive scrawled across it. A feud between Franco and *YDN* ensued. Cohen eventually retracted her critique, saying she was a fan who respected Franco and hoped there would be no ill will. Franco never commented on the *YDN*'s coverage of him again, and his Twitter account was canceled soon after.

Franco and the Yale Daily News exchanged heated comments on Twitter after the student newspaper criticized a photo from Franco's hosting of the 83rd Academy Awards with Anne Hathaway.

Though off-the-cuff criticism of the actor has not shown up again on the blog, articles continue to be written about him. In late 2011 several articles asked where Franco had gone, since he was no longer regularly seen on campus. One blog post said, "Maybe we're being a little presumptuous, but we're worried our very public spat with Franco may have soured his impression of Yale. We'd take it all back for one more uncomfortable encounter at Starbucks or weird doubletake on the train to Boston. We guess this is all to say: Come back to us, James. We miss u."

Marissa Medansky. "Where Have All the Francos Gone?" *Yale Daily News*, October 31, 2011. www.yaledailynews.com/news/2011/oct/31/where-have-all-francos-gone.

For these reasons, other students and professors are often eager to work with Franco on extracurricular projects. When Franco tossed around ideas with another student at Yale about creating a student musical that Franco would produce and direct, for example, people lined up to make it happen. When Franco wanted to star in a movie written by one of his NYU professors, that professor was more than willing to let Rabbit Bandini Productions create the film.

Franco also hardly gets through life like a normal student. He manages the details of his many projects, programs, and classes by relying on his assistant, Dana Morgan. Morgan, a former UCLA classmate, manages Franco's daily life. Morgan says, "I tease him when people say, 'How do you do it?' You don't! You do all the things they know about, but you don't do the normal human-being things.'"[63] Morgan ensures that Franco wakes up, gets to the places he needs to go, has clean laundry, and eats. When Franco needs to meet with a professor or must find time to collaborate with another student for class, Morgan is the one who arranges the meeting, which might take place in person, through a video conference, or even on the commuter train.

Another source of Franco's productivity is that he sleeps as little as possible. Franco says, "I don't even like to sleep—I feel as if there's too much to do."[64] He gets a few hours of sleep a night, then relies on catnaps whenever he can find them. He is able to fall asleep nearly anywhere, at any second, and has even been known sometimes to nod off in the middle of a conversation. "I have a lot of interests and a lot I want to get done, so I've gotten into the habit of not getting into my bed," he says. "I have the computer in a protective case because it often ends up falling to the floor."[65]

Going back to school reinvigorated Franco and allowed him to explore many more sides of himself than acting. Though his personal schedule seems extreme, it is clear that he loves school. "I go to school because I love being around people who are interested in what I'm interested in, and I'm having a great experience,"[66] he says. Indeed, class is exactly where Franco wants to be; he does not plan to let up anytime soon, even as his Hollywood career grows to include bigger and better projects.

Chapter 4

Multitasking Franco

James Franco is fascinated by art in all its forms. In part because of his celebrity, he has had the chance to study art and try his hand at numerous creative art forms, such as writing, filmmaking, visual arts, and performance art. These endeavors have attracted as much attention as they have criticism. Franco maintains that rather than perfecting any one form of art, he is most passionate about exploring how different art forms intersect.

Filmmaking

Through his production company, Rabbit Bandini Productions, Franco hoped to produce and direct independent films. At NYU's filmmaking program, he embraced this interest and began to churn out such projects, many of which got their start as class assignments.

In December 2008, just two months after enrolling in his first semester at NYU, Franco began work on a documentary about *Saturday Night Live* (*SNL*), the famous sketch comedy show that airs on television each week. Franco had hosted *SNL* a few months earlier and found the experience fascinating. For a class assignment, Franco needed to create a short film; he planned to focus on Bill Hader, one of the *SNL* actors. After hosting his episode, Franco approached Lorne Michaels, the producer of the show, for permission to follow Hader for the assignment. Michaels did one

The 2010 documentary, Saturday Night, *was crafted by James Franco as a behind-the-scenes look at the late night, popular, comedy show* Saturday Night Live. *It met with much critical praise when released at independent film festivals.*

step better, however: He invited Franco and his partners, Vince Jolivette and Miles Levy, to follow the development of an entire episode, which takes a week.

Intrigued, Franco filmed the week leading up to the December 6, 2008, episode, hosted by John Malkovich. Franco filmed everything, including the comedy writers' initial pitches for sketches; set construction for the live broadcast; and the broadcast itself. He interviewed the actors, writers, and backstage staff. The resulting documentary was shown at several independent film festivals in 2010, including the South by Southwest Film Festival in Austin, Texas, and the Tribeca Film Festival in New York City.

The film received lots of attention, largely because of the interest audiences had in the topic. *SNL* is one of the longest-running shows on television, but it takes place behind very closed doors. Many critics reviewed the documentary favorably. Calling it "unintentionally fascinating," one critic for the *Los Angeles Weekly* wrote, "*Saturday Night* is fascinating and absolutely worth seeing, but for what are probably the wrong reasons."[67] In her view,

Playing Gay

Pop-culture magazines and blogs love to speculate about James Franco's sexuality, in part because he has played a number of gay characters. He played Harvey Milk's boyfriend in the movie *Milk* and also portrayed the gay poets Allen Ginsberg (in *Howl*) and Hart Crane (in *The Broken Tower*). Though he is not gay, Franco says he is interested in playing gay characters because he finds their struggles deeply compelling. He explains:

Actors Sean Penn, left, and James Franco in a scene from the 2008 film Milk, *in which Franco played a gay character. It was one of several gay roles in Franco's career.*

> There are lots of other reasons to be interested in gay characters than wanting myself to go out and have sex with guys. ... I've played a gay man who's living in the '60s and '70s, a gay man who we depicted in the '50s, and one being in the '20s. And those were all periods when to be gay, at least being gay in public, was much more difficult. Part of what I'm interested in is how these people who were living anti-normative lifestyles contended with opposition.

Quoted in Keith Staskiewicz. "James Franco on Playing Gay Characters: 'You Know What, Maybe I'm Just Gay.'" *EW.com*, January 5, 2011. http://insidemovies.ew.com/2011/01/05/james-franco-gay-roles.

what made the movie fascinating had little to do with Franco's directing and filmmaking skills and more to do with surprising revelations by the *SNL* actors and writers. Nonetheless, the movie did well at each film festival and gave Franco credibility as a director.

In 2010 Franco had more than one film showing at the Tribeca Film Festival: He was also premiering the film *William Vincent*. Franco made use of his NYU connections for this film, which was written, directed, and edited by his NYU directing professor and head of the department, Jay Anania. Jolivette and Franco approached Anania after Franco's first year at NYU to create a film specifically for Franco to star in and produce. The film was inspired by a Japanese book on aesthetics, a branch of philosophy that is concerned with the nature of art and beauty, called *In Praise of Shadows*. Even though the film received mixed reviews, it offered Franco more experience on the independent film festival circuit, where he would continue to introduce a number of other class projects turned professional films.

Poetry on Film

Franco also began to adapt poetry, or stories about poets, to film. For NYU class assignments, he made three short films and one full-length feature based on individual poems and poets.

Franco had cultivated an interest in contemporary poetry while at UCLA and had always toyed with the idea of taking one of his favorite poems by Anthony Hecht to film. An NYU assignment was the perfect vehicle. He adapted one of Hecht's poems, "The Feast of Stephen," for his first film because the poem struck him as particularly cinematic. Franco also created a short film based on "Herbert White," a poem by Frank Bidart; and another on "The Clerk's Tale," by Spencer Reece. Franco submitted at least two of the films to independent festivals. *The Clerk's Tale* premiered at the 2010 Cannes Film Festival, while *The Feast of Stephen* was shown at the Berlin International Film Festival, the Chicago International Film Festival, and several others.

Creating these short films prepared Franco to make a full-length film, which became his thesis project, a graduation requirement from the NYU filmmaking program. While at UCLA, Franco became interested in the poet Hart Crane and a biography of his life called *The Broken Tower* (2011). Crane was a conflicted gay man who lived a highly dramatic life. He eventually died by committing suicide at sea. Crane's poetry is filled with metaphors and notoriously difficult

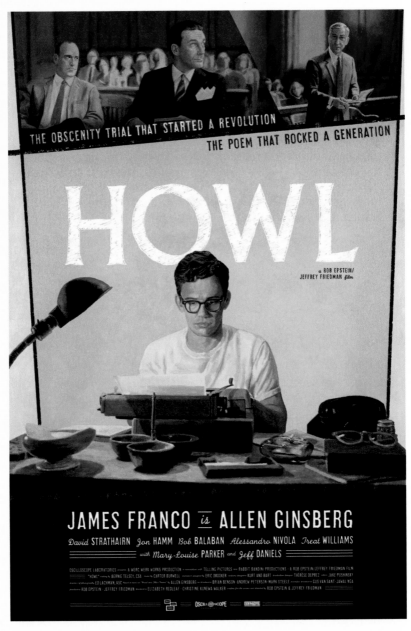

THE OBSCENITY TRIAL THAT STARTED A REVOLUTION

THE POEM THAT ROCKED A GENERATION

HOWL

a ROB EPSTEIN/
JEFFREY FRIEDMAN film

JAMES FRANCO *is* ALLEN GINSBERG

David STRATHAIRN *Jon* HAMM *Bob* BALABAN *Alessandro* NIVOLA *Treat* WILLIAMS

with Mary-Louise PARKER *and Jeff* DANIELS

James Franco was cast as the lead in the 2010 movie Howl, about beat-era poet Allen Ginsburg. He was excited about the role and immediately set about immersing himself in everything Ginsberg.

Photography

James Franco has also tried his hand at photography. In 2011 he signed with the clothing company 7 for All Mankind to direct and photograph their spring ad campaign. He also shot a series of photographs of actress Agyness Deyn for an editorial layout in *Elle* magazine and another series of photographs for *W* magazine. The way in which photos tell stories is what Franco says attracts him to the medium.

to understand. Franco's goal was to make a film that captured his writing style. To this end, his movie (in which he starred as Crane) featured a series of unsettling scenes that captured Crane's depressive lows, drunken rages, sex life, and literary endeavors.

At times the movie moves at a fast clip, shifting quickly between somewhat unrelated scenes; at other times it has a slower pace. When it was shown at film festivals in 2011, it received mixed reviews. Franco, however, was unconcerned. For example, a movie critic in attendance at the Los Angeles Film Festival wrote, "Franco acknowledged that his movie required patience and engagement from the audience. ('Thank you for staying,' he joked right after the screening.) But he was unapologetic about the way he chose to shoot the film."[68] Franco compared the film's reception to the reception Crane's poetry received during his life. "Crane said, 'If I just have six good readers, that's enough for me,'" Franco said. "But I hope people with the same tastes as mine would enjoy it."[69]

In addition to making his own films about poets, Franco was also cast as famous beat-era poet Allen Ginsberg in *Howl*, a 2010 feature-length film by professional filmmakers Jeffrey Friedman and Rob Epstein. *Howl* follows Ginsberg through the 1957 obscenity trial he faced after publishing his famous poem of the same name.

Franco was so excited about the project that he agreed to the role and began embodying the character of Ginsberg before the producers had even secured funding for the project. To become Ginsberg, Franco wore big, black glasses and listened to recordings of Ginsberg's poetry readings on his iPod on the way to class through the New York subway. Franco read biographies of the poet, watched interviews, and talked to experts on Ginsberg's poetry to immerse himself fully in the character.

Though Franco bore little resemblance to the real-life Ginsberg, the directors saw something similar between the two. "I have joked that he's a 21st-century beatnik," said Epstein, "but he really does have that sensibility. He's really interested and excited about experimentation and exploring the possibilities of how one can be an artist."[70]

Published Author

Franco's NYU work was not the only fodder for his projects; he also found wider audiences for the creative writing he developed in his classes at Columbia and Brooklyn College. A few of the stories Franco wrote as class assignments were published in 2010 issues of the literary magazine *McSweeney's* and also in *Esquire* magazine.

That same year, book publisher Scribner released a collection of Franco's short stories, called *Palo Alto* after Franco's hometown in California. The stories, which were inspired by Franco's own adolescence, follow the life experiences of fictional teenagers. Like many of Franco's other projects, the book received mixed reviews. "It's evident in *Palo Alto* that Franco has worked on his craft, and at times he displays surprising talent," noted critic Oscar Villalon in the *San Francisco Weekly*. However, Villalon added that "these stories, in the end, just don't add up to much … These young screwed up lives are worth looking at, but their stories don't hold any weight."[71] Another recurring critique was that Franco was not as good a writer as he was an actor or filmmaker. "With 'Palo Alto,' Franco's literary execution hasn't quite matched his other performances,"[72] observed Joshua Mohr in the *New York Times*.

Franco was largely unaffected by the less-than-stellar reviews. "I never said I was going to be the best author," he said. "I'm just trying to, you know, write the best book that I can. … I'm happy at the level I aimed at."[73] At least a few others agreed with him: By 2012 he had lined up another book deal. Amazon Publishing agreed to publish his first novel, titled *Actors Anonymous*, which is scheduled for release in 2013.

Perhaps because he is a celebrity, Franco is less concerned than other artists with the commercial success of his projects. "As hard as I work in film, it's my day job," he said. "[The poetry projects and writing] are, I don't know, pure expression."[74]

General Hospital

In yet another expressive exercise, in 2009 Franco made the unusual move of approaching *General Hospital*, a daytime soap opera, and asking that a role be created for him. His only conditions for appearing on the show were that his character had to be an artist and had to be crazy. *General Hospital* executives jumped at the idea. Jill Farren-Phelps, the executive producer of the show, said of Franco's turn on the show, "We think it has sort of a cool factor that definitely freshens the image of daytime."[75] Soap operas in general have been slipping in popularity, and several of the longest-running shows have experienced severe declines in viewership or have been canceled.

Franco got the idea on a different set when he toyed with the idea of playing a character that was a soap opera actor. From there, he began imagining what would happen if he actually *became* an actor on a soap opera. The idea struck him as interesting because of the perception that soap operas are a lower form of cinematic art. He thought appearing on the show would be a great way to experiment with performance art, an abstract art medium in which he is keenly interested. Franco says he loves how performance art allows artists to "[put] down their paintbrushes and cameras and [turn] to their bodies as instruments."[76]

Franco jumped into his experiment by signing on to perform in twenty episodes of *General Hospital* as a bad boy artist named Franco. He loved the idea that his appearance would challenge the audience's ability to see him not as famous Hollywood actor James Franco, but as the character Franco on the show. As he put it:

Franco explored all mediums of art, and in 2009 he accepted a role as a mysterious artist on the long-running soap opera General Hospital.

I disrupted the audience's suspension of disbelief, because no matter how far I got into the character, I was going to be perceived as something that doesn't belong to the incredibly stylized world of soap operas. Everyone watching would see an actor they recognized, a real person in a made-up world. In performance art, the outcome is uncertain—and this was no exception. My hope was for people to ask themselves if soap operas are really that far from entertainment that is considered critically legitimate. Whether they did was out of my hands.[77]

To further complicate the experiment, one of Franco's episodes took place in a Los Angeles art museum. The episode showed Franco putting on an art exhibit. It was taped live at the Museum of Contemporary Art (MOCA) in an event that was a part of a real art exhibit, called *SOAP at MOCA*. The episode, filmed for television, featured the real museum director, Jeffrey Dietrich, as well as other real-life artists. Prominent performance artists attended the live taping of the episode, as well as a real-life exhibit. The many layers of the project—artists watching artists play artists on a television show—excited Franco, as did people's responses.

Gucci

James Franco became the face of Gucci cologne in 2008 and appeared in a number of print advertisements and television commercials for the brand. He viewed his work as ironic, since he was once caught shoplifting men's cologne while in high school. Gucci became Franco's official formal outfitter, dressing him for all his formal events since 2009, including when he hosted the Academy Awards in 2011. In 2011 Franco became the face of Gucci's made-to-measure suit service, which allows customers to have a suit custom-made to their exact measurements.

"I didn't know what would happen," said Franco. "But what did happen is there was a huge reaction. People said, 'What is he doing?' You know, big papers … started writing about a soap opera. And so I realized wow. … People are looking at this with fresh eyes. There has been a rupture."[78]

The Dangerous Book Four Boys

The aspect of his *General Hospital* stint that most excited Franco was the experimental nature of the project, as well as the way in which he pushed the boundaries between different art forms. This was true of another art form Franco pursued: painting. Although painting was the first art form Franco ever tried his hand at, it was not until 2010 that he began to create art that combined painting and drawing with film and video.

In June 2010 Franco launched his first solo art show, called *The Dangerous Book Four Boys*, in the Clocktower Gallery in New York City. The name of the show was a riff on the book *The Dangerous Book for Boys*, an ironic how-to book of stereotypical boy activities. As a part of the show, Franco tore pages out of the book, doodled on them, framed them, and hung them all over the gallery. The show included an assortment of media: films, photos, framed doodles, and wooden structures. The theme that united it all was the idea that the transition from boyhood to adolescence is a messy one. There was a special emphasis on violence and sex. Much of the art was explicitly obscene or violent. One video included monologues about rape, murder, and diarrhea and also featured images of a penis urinating and an anus defecating. Another short film, called *Dicknose in Paris*, showed Franco, as the main character, wearing a prosthetic penis in the middle of his face as he walked around the capital of France.

Like much of his work, reviews were mixed. One of Franco's own professors, who saw an early version of the show, found his videos extremely offensive, particularly *Dicknose in Paris*. Franco chalked her opinion up to not having seen the video in the context of the larger show. *New York Times* art critic Roberta Smith found the show's many videos and images hard to sort through, though she did find some images poignant. Nonetheless, Smith wrote, "The show is a confusing mix of the clueless and the halfway promising."[79]

In 2010 Franco launched a solo art show called The Dangerous Book Four Boys, *an ironic how-to book and experimental exhibit that received very mixed reviews.*

Invisible Art

If reviewers found *The Dangerous Book Four Boys* confusing, they were even more baffled by his next endeavor. Continuing his experiment with visual art, in 2011 Franco partnered with two other artists to create what they call the Museum of Non-visible Art. The museum, which describes itself as an "extravagance of imagination,"[80] displays different pieces of invisible art, each of which is described in words on a small plaque. There is no physical artwork, only plaques titling and describing the imagined invisible art. All of the pieces are for sale, and prices range from twenty dollars to ten thousand dollars.

One piece by Franco is an invisible film called *Red Leaves*. Available for twenty-five dollars, Franco describes the film as "a portrait of a culture on the brink of extinction" and says it is based on a William Faulkner story. In a video promotion for the museum, Franco says, "I originally intended this to be a film that would go to festivals, but it got so expensive, you know, the budget was so high back then that I never realized it. So I've finally been able to realize it for this museum and now I consider it a piece of art."[81] Other works by Franco include a costume for the film (fifty dollars) and a sculpture (one hundred dollars).

Much of the press covering the Museum of Non-visible Art maintained a tongue-in-cheek tone that laughed at the concept of non-visible artwork. Annie Vaughan of Fox News wrote, "[Franco's] nifty trick in the art world is finding a way to be an artist without actually executing a physical work."[82] Others were more direct, like Emma Mustich of *Salon.com*, who wrote, "James Franco's newest art project is either an example of subtle creativity, an extremely shallow con, or a hoax."[83] Franco's involvement in the museum confirmed the suspicions of many who had long doubted Franco's foray into the world of art.

Franco insists, however, that non-visible art, and all art, is consistent with his drive to experience and experiment with different art forms and how they relate to one another. "I like the idea of being able to tell, you know, deliver my subject matter in the best form possible," he says. "I like that freedom. But I also like the idea of examining how these different forms of mediums interact. ... How they blend. What their limitations are."[84] It is certainly clear that James Franco puts no limits on what he can create.

Chapter 5

Who Is the Real James Franco?

The wide array of Franco's projects and programs has generated much discussion of his intentions and abilities. His frantic output has been characterized as either the work of a creative genius or a professional phony. Some think he genuinely views his entire life—his roles, oddball art installations, and public behavior—as performance art, while others write him off as an attention-hungry actor. The truth is that James Franco largely has not yet made sense of himself, nor does he feel the need to.

Multihyphenate

Not since 2006 has Franco been just an actor. Journalists have taken to calling Franco a "multihyphenate" to describe his identity as an actor-student-director-artist-writer-photographer. Interviewers, fans, and critics all seem to want to know why Franco feels compelled to do all of these things, and why all at once? It is not unusual for celebrities to devote themselves to very specific causes or hobbies, such as devout veganism or adopting children from third world countries. Yet Franco is alone in approaching his non-Hollywood endeavors with more ferocity than he does his acting career.

Franco explains himself simply by saying he is not content with being only an actor. He feels fortunate to make his living by acting but sees no reason that line of work should preclude

Journalists have taken to calling James Franco a "multihyphenate" to describe his identity as an actor, student, director, artist, writer, and photographer. Here, Franco arrives at the Los Angeles Museum of Contemporary Art in 2012 for its presentation of "Rebel," an artistic effort that Franco conceived.

him from others. "One of the reasons I am engaged in different disciplines and outlets is I don't like feeling trapped in one thing," he says. "And by trapped, I mean when all I had was acting, the best that I could ask for was a great role and to become the best actor that I could be. But to my mind, that's limited."[85]

While some are impressed with Franco's manic school attendance, film project productivity, and artistic explorations, others deeply question his sincerity and accuse him of piling too much on his plate. As Sam Anderson, the *New York* magazine writer who followed Franco for an in-depth profile in 2011, put it, "Is he genuinely trying to improve himself or is he just messing with us—using celebrity itself as the raw material for some kind of public prank?"[86] Bloggers, journalists, and gossip magazines have become keen on answering this question, with some portraying Franco as a creative genius and others regarding him as a phony.

Franco says he is simply taking advantage of the opportunity to explore all the things he wants to while he can do it. Early on in his filmmaking, before he even attended NYU, Franco made a short video about a little boy grappling with the idea of mortality after his goldfish dies. Even though the boy's parents tell him not to worry because he has lots of time, the boy is not comforted. He begins to feel he must accomplish everything he wants as quickly as possible.

Clearly echoed in this story is the four-year-old Franco, who told his parents he did not want to die because he had so much to do, and this is how Franco answers critics who accuse him of stretching himself too thin by pursuing too many things at once. "If the work is good," Franco asks, "What does it matter? I'm doing it because I love it. Why not do as many things I love as I can? As long as the work is good."[87] Above all, Franco rejects suggestions that his frenetic output is just a way to add notches to his artistic belt. "For me, it's not like, 'Well, I've ticked THAT off my list,'" He says. "It's just searching for the right kind of outlet for each subject matter or form of expression."[88]

It could just be that Franco increasingly views his entire life as an ongoing piece of performance art. *127 Hours* director Danny Boyle believes this to be the case. "He's turned his celebrity into a form of performance art," Boyle says. "While we were shooting the film, he would sometimes ask me, "What do you want him to do?" I would say, What do you mean? He would say, "What do you want from him in this scene?" You mean your character? "No, no. Franco. What do you want from Franco?" He was talking about himself in the third person."[89]

Who Is James Franco?

Perhaps one of the most perplexing things about Franco's multipronged existence is that it lacks a clear goal. He often seems spread in a million directions, and for all of the connections and collaborations he loves to make, many of his projects seem

People who meet Franco for the first time often describe him as aloof, tired, and in possession of a piercing stare. He quickly relaxes, however, and proves to be quite engaging.

Cat Person

James Franco loves cats. He likes to name his cats after figures in literature, and his current two cats are named Zelda, after writer Zelda Fitzgerald (wife of F. Scott Fitzgerald); and Sammy, after Sammy Glick, the main character in the novel *What Makes Sammy Run?* by Budd Schulberg. Franco often brags about his cats in interviews. "They're very loving and have great personalities. Said like a true cat owner," he laughed.

Quoted in Julie Hinds. "James Franco Appreciates Chances to Push Boundaries." *Houston Chronicle*, August 7, 2011.

disjointed and unconnected, as does his true identity. Even journalists who have spent weeks shadowing him and have been privy to the ins and outs of his daily rhythms have a hard time coming to a coherent characterization of who he truly is.

Upon first meetings, Franco often seems aloof and tired, yet he maintains an almost uncomfortable level of eye contact. However, a short time into the meeting, he will break his own ice, say something disarming, and suddenly smile broadly. Boyle shares the following first impression of Franco: "When we first met him, we thought he was stoned. I remember speaking to a casting director at Fox and she said, 'Don't be put off by that. He does that to keep you at a distance at the beginning, so that he can suss [figure] you out.' You think he's sleeping, but in fact he's hyperactive. He never rests."[90]

In person and in interviews, Franco is a confusing mix of characteristics. He comes across as both earnest and contriving. He portrays himself as simultaneously open and mysterious. He might respond to questions with complicated, high-minded answers or come across as down-to-earth. Franco says that much of the dissonance has to do with the fact that he is at heart a shy person who used to dislike talking about himself. Franco especially did not enjoy talking about projects that he was not proud of. He grappled with this for a while, until he talked to a painter friend who told him that he never minded giving interviews because he loved his work, so interviews were simply a chance to talk about something he loved. For Franco that idea clicked. "Now that I'm engaged with a lot of other things that I'm interested in, I don't mind talking," he says. "It also feels less like I'm just selling a studio's product and more like I can just have discussions about things that I enjoy."[91]

"Part of the Conversation"

It seems clear that Franco is still figuring out exactly who he is. Many of his projects focus on adolescence, that phase of defining and discovering one's self. Part of his multitasking is also a result of the deep unhappiness he felt when his entire life was about making movies. "When all I had was acting, despite telling myself that it's the wrong kind of thinking, I would define myself by the movies I did," he says. "If the movie did well, I would feel happy and if it didn't, I would get upset."[92] He has become a much happier person by having a number of interests to keep him busy, by defining himself as an artist who acts, rather than just as an actor. Now that he identifies himself broadly as an artist, he says he is much happier, even if onlookers are confused.

While many wonder when Franco will settle into a more stable career, he is not interested in limiting himself to just one or two of his interests. He is unconcerned with perfecting his skills in any one art form. More important to him is that he continue to explore different avenues of art, and especially to collaborate with others. "More and more, I would say, I look for opportunities to collaborate with people. So whether I'm directing, or doing an art show, or acting in a film, I am most inspired when I am collaborating with someone," he says. "So I don't necessarily like to be my own boss. I think what I like is to be part of the conversation, all the way through the piece."[93]

Professor James Franco

When asked about his goals and where he sees himself in ten years, James Franco says he hopes to do more of everything—more acting, more art, and more school. The latter, however, he plans to approach from the front of the classroom: Franco is already working on a PhD and hopes one day to become a professor.

During the 2011 fall semester, Franco got his first experience teaching. With support from NYU, Franco taught his first class, a poetry and filmmaking workshop. The class was made up of eight students handpicked by Franco. Together they made a feature-length film based on a book of contemporary poetry. "I kind of see that [project] as a way to give deserving students an opportunity to actually make something and give them the opportunities that I was given," Franco said of the experience.

Quoted in Adam Ranthe. "James Franco, NYU Professor, Reveals Details of His Class; Students Will Transfer Poetry to Film." *New York Daily News*, August 3, 2011. http://articles.nydailynews.com/2011-08-03/gossip/29862426_1_kanbar-institute-nyu-students-nyu-professor.

Media Obsessed?

The media has followed Franco's many incarnations with keen interest. Each time he announces or premieres a new project, the news is headlined, blogged, and otherwise discussed. The public has closely followed his actions since he decided to go back to school in 2006.

Franco is surprised his ventures into academia and art have been newsworthy and is confused about why his efforts have

Franco receives a Spirit Award from Film Independent in 2009. The media follows all of Franco's activities with much interest, and some have accused that his actions are all designed to seek out that attention.

attracted such criticism. While others characterize him as attention seeking, Franco is clear he did not return to school to get articles written about him. "I'm actually taking [school] extremely seriously," he insists. "It's a weird thing that's happened because my school life now has turned into something else where it's got this focus on it, almost as if it was this other performance, or a side of my career."[94] Going to school, doing his work, making some art, and creating new films are all projects he says he takes seriously. They are not the publicity antics some make them out to be.

Nonetheless, many of Franco's project topics, interview answers, and even personal life choices seem designed to grab people's attention. After filming three movies in which he played gay men, Franco defused speculation that he is gay by explaining that such characters' depth and struggle appeal to him—then turned around and reignited speculation by saying, "Or, you know what, maybe I'm just gay."[95]

At times, Franco borders on bizarre and self-absorbed. For example, he once brought a Polaroid camera and multiple boxes of film to an interview and encouraged the interviewer to document everything, including what he ordered for breakfast. A different time, while teaching an editing seminar at a film school in California, his students' project was to edit images of him. (In fact, the name of the seminar was Editing James Franco—with James Franco.) While at Yale he started plans to produce a musical called *James Franco Presents*, which was about James Franco producing a musical.

This narcissism, combined with his obsessively ambitious schedule, has prompted people to make fun of him. *New York* magazine journalist Sam Anderson sarcastically quipped that up next for Franco is to "become president of the United Nations, train a flock of African gray parrots to perform free colonoscopies in the developing world, and launch himself into space in order to explain the human heart to aliens living at the pulsing core of interstellar quasars."[96]

Franco seems to delight in keeping the media on their toes, guessing what he will do next and what it all means. "The press are going to come up with an image of you no matter what," he says, "so if projects like *General Hospital* are a way to go out there and shake that up a little bit I don't see the harm."[97]

His Biggest Roles Yet

Despite the fact that he is sometimes ridiculed, Franco's unique and disparate interests have provided him a secure, if peculiar, place in Hollywood. Franco only began to be offered his favorite, multidimensional movie roles after he immersed himself in school and other artistic projects. With *Pineapple Express*, *Milk*, and a series of cameo roles as himself in popular movies like *Knocked Up* and *Eat, Pray, Love*, Franco has become an interesting and edgy person in Hollywood, known for much more than just his pretty face.

In addition, becoming known for his artistic output and academic strivings has helped him become the kind of actor who can be immune to the pressure of steering a Hollywood career.

While Franco's pursuits have grown, he has always continued to act. His leading role in the 2010 film **127 Hours** *was critically acclaimed and may be one of his biggest roles to date.*

As friend and fellow actor Seth Rogen puts it, "I think when he went off to school, it gave him permission not to take [acting] so seriously, and when you approach it like that you start doing a lot better stuff than when the weight of the world is on every acting choice you make."[98]

By taking acting less seriously, Franco ironically found himself cast in his biggest movies yet. In 2010 he starred in *127 Hours*, an adventure film about the true story of a mountain climber who

Franco to Play Robert Mapplethorpe

In 2012 James Franco earned the opportunity to play the role in another biopic about an artist who died young. He was cast as Robert Mapplethorpe, the controversial photographer who was as well known for photographing a number of Hollywood icons, including as Andy Warhol and Richard Gere, as he was for his more explicitly sexual photos that many argued were obscene.

Robert Mapplethorpe was a controversial photographer who took photos of many Hollywood icons. In 2012 Franco was cast as the lead in an upcoming biopic about the photographer.

Mapplethorpe died of complications from AIDS in 1989. The film project is being funded by a grant from the Tribeca All Access program, which provides fifteen thousand dollars to eleven different projects to connect aspiring filmmakers with professionals in the industry. The film will be the first narrative project by documentary director Ondi Timoner.

cuts off his own arm to save his life. The movie was significant because it featured few other actors and little action; most of the movie was a close-up of Franco's face as he struggles with his predicament, trapped deep in a canyon in Utah.

Franco's performance was so impressive that it earned him a nomination for an Academy Award for Best Actor. Reviewer Bill Goodykoontz was one person who applauded Franco's performance, writing, "Franco always has been good; here he's great, navigating the transition from cocky outsider to a dying man desperate to belong—to belong to something, to his family, to the universe, to anything."[99] Film critic A.O. Scott agrees, crediting Franco with the movie's success. "How do you turn an immobilized protagonist into the hero of a motion picture, emphasis on motion?" he asked. "The most obvious answer is that you cast James Franco, an actor whose loose physicality and free-ranging intelligence make him good company for a lonely spell in wilderness."[100]

In 2011 Franco played the scientist in *Rise of the Planet of the Apes*. The movie was intended to be a reboot of the film series *Planet of the Apes,* which were released during the late 1960s and early 1970s. At first Franco was uninterested in the role, but he had a change of heart when he learned that advanced technology would be used to create the apes in the movie. Actor Andy Serkis played the main ape; the advanced technology turned his movements and actions into the human-like ape seen on the big screen. "I was interested in this kind of CG [computer-generated] work now because it's different than it was in the past when actors had to act opposite tennis balls," he said. "Here was now a chance to use these high level of effects but be able to have an old-fashioned acting experience where it's one actor opposite another."[101] The movie was both a box office and critical success, one of the most popular movies that summer.

In 2012 Franco earned a role in *Oz: The Great and Powerful*, a big-budget Disney prequel to the 1939 classic *The Wizard of Oz.* Franco played the young wizard Oz, another sign of his enigmatic place in Hollywood. The movie was slated for release in March 2013. Also in 2012 Franco was still hyperactively pursuing academia. He continued his PhD work at Yale, gained entrance to

In 2011 Franco took on the role of a scientist in the movie **Rise of the Planet of the Apes.** *He was excited about working on a film that used computer-generated technology to depict the apes in the movie.*

a PhD program at the University of Houston, and added more classes at the Rhode Island School of Design. On top of all this, he continued to produce, write, and direct a number of independent films for the independent film circuit.

Indeed, Franco's multitasking, multihyphenate career shows no signs of slowing down. Whether to ogle his Gucci-endorsing movie star looks, marvel at his productivity, revel in his artistic expression, criticize his work, or gossip about his life's truths or fictions, America seems unable to look away from the celebrity that is James Franco, and that is just fine with him.

Notes

Introduction: Hollywood's Renaissance Man

1. Sam Anderson. "The James Franco Project." *New York*, July 25, 2010. http://nymag.com/movies/profiles/67284.
2. Anderson. "The James Franco Project."
3. Anderson. "The James Franco Project."
4. Quoted in *Charlie Rose*. "James Franco." Video. May 6, 2011. www.charlierose.com/view/interview/11661.
5. Quoted in *Charlie Rose*. "James Franco."

Chapter 1: Breaking Expectations

6. Quoted in Lindsey Soll. "10 Things You Don't Know About James Franco." *EW.com*, September 29, 2006. www.ew.com/ew/article/0,,1540514,00.html.
7. Quoted in Jill Wolfson. "Penciling in a Career: In Children's Books, Betsy Franco Found the Career That Worked with Motherhood." *Stanford Magazine*, September/October 2009. www.stanfordalumni.org/news/magazine/2009/sepoct/show/franco.html.
8. Quoted in Melena Ryzik. "James Franco's (Extremely) Creative Ferment." *New York Times.com*, September 8, 2010. www.nytimes.com/2010/09/12/movies/12ryzik.html?pagewanted=all.
9. Quoted in Anderson. "The James Franco Project."
10. Quoted in *Inside the Actors Studio*. "James Franco: On Acting." Bravo TV.com, December 7, 2010.
11. Quoted in Kristy Davis. "Books That Made a Difference to James Franco." Oprah.com, November 22, 2010. www.oprah.com/omagazine/Books-That-Made-a-Difference-to-James-Franco.
12. Quoted in Amy Raphael. "Acting Clever." *Guardian* (UK), January 23, 2009. www.guardian.co.uk/film/2009/jan/24/james-franco-interview-milk.

13. Quoted in *Inside the Actors Studio*. "James Franco."
14. Quoted in *Inside the Actors Studio*. "James Franco."
15. Quoted in *Inside the Actors Studio*. "James Franco."
16. Quoted in *Charlie Rose*. "James Franco."
17. Quoted in Cindy Pearlman. "Making Big Screen via Big Macs: James Franco Takes Orders a Little Differently Now." *Chicago Sun-Times*, January 22, 2006.
18. Quoted in Astri von Arbin Ahlander. "James Franco." Days of Yore. www.thedaysofyore.com/james-franco.
19. Quoted in Ahlander. "James Franco."
20. Quoted in Ahlander. "James Franco."
21. Quoted in Ahlander. "James Franco."
22. Quoted in Pearlman. "Making Big Screen via Big Macs."
23. Quoted in Joyce Chen. "James Franco Credits Obsession, UCLA Education, Giving Back for Success: 'Inside the Actors Studio.'" *NY Daily News*, December 8, 2010. http://articles.nydailynews.com/2010-12-08/entertainment/27083812_1_actors-studio-james-lipton-james-franco.

Chapter 2: Disappearing Franco

24. Quoted in Willem Dafoe. "The Real McCoy: James Franco." *Interview*, February 2006.
25. Quoted in Amy Kaufman. "Judd Apatow's 'Freaks and Geeks' Gang Reminisces—and Mocks James Franco." *Los Angeles Times*, March 14, 2011. http://latimesblogs.latimes.com/showtracker/2011/03/freaks-and-geeks-paley-fest-judd-apatow-james-franco-jason-segel-seth-rogen.html.
26. Quoted in *Morning Edition*. "James Franco Doesn't Limit Himself to Acting." National Public Radio, October 15, 2010. www.npr.org/templates/story/story.php?storyId=130582431.
27. Quoted in Ryzik. "James Franco's (Extremely) Creative Ferment."
28. Quoted in Kelly Carter. "James Franco: The Next James Dean." *USA Today*, June 26, 2001. www.usatoday.com/life/television/2001-07-27-james-franco.htm.
29. Quoted in Carter. "James Franco."

30. Quoted in Cindy Pearlman. "Young Actor Answers the Call of the 'Sea,'" *Chicago Sun-Times*, September 4, 2002.
31. Quoted in Cindy Pearlman. "Young Actor Answers the Call of the 'Sea.'"
32. Quoted in Evan Henerson. "Addicted to Acting: A Passion for His Work Takes 'City by the Sea's' James Franco to Extremes." *Los Angeles Daily News*, September 6, 2002.
33. Quoted in Pearlman. "Young Actor Answers the Call of the 'Sea.'"
34. Quoted in Nicolas Cage. "James Franco." *Interview*, February 2003.
35. Quoted in Henerson. "Addicted to Acting."
36. Quoted in *Charlie Rose*. "James Franco."
37. Quoted in Henerson. "Addicted to Acting."
38. Quoted in Angela Dawson. "Franco Takes Pride in 'Flyboys' Reality." *Chicago Sun-Times*, September 29, 2006.
39. Quoted in Dafoe. "The Real McCoy."
40. Stephanie Zacharek. "Annapolis." *Salon.com*, January 27, 2006. www.salon.com/2006/01/27/annapolis_2.
41. Michael Phillips. "'Flyboys' Fails to Reach a Higher Plane." *Los Angeles Times*, September 22, 2006. http://articles.latimes.com/2006/sep/22/entertainment/et-flyboys22.
42. Quoted in *Charlie Rose*. "James Franco."
43. Quoted in *Charlie Rose*. "James Franco."
44. Quoted in Tom Shone. "A Class Apart: An Interview with James Franco." *Telegraph* (UK), January 4, 2011. www.telegraph.co.uk/culture/film/starsandstories/8209459/A-class-apart-interview-with-James-Franco.html.
45. Quoted in *Charlie Rose*. "James Franco."

Chapter 3: The Actor Goes Back to School

46. Quoted in Randi Schmelzer. "Smart Set." *UCLA Magazine*, January 1, 2009. http://magazine.ucla.edu/features/smart_set.
47. Quoted in Schmelzer. "Smart Set."

48. Quoted in *Morning Edition*. "James Franco Doesn't Limit Himself to Acting."
49. Michael Phillips. "'Pineapple Express' Stars James Franco, Seth Rogen." *Chicago Tribune*, August 6, 2008. www.chicagotribune.com/features/chi-pineapple-express-0806aug06,0,5842152.story.
50. Andrew Schenker and Sal Cinquemani. "*Pineapple Express.*" *Slant*, January 3, 2009. www.slantmagazine.com/dvd/review/pineapple-express/1446.
51. Quoted in Donna Freydkin. "James Franco Digs Deep: Versatile Actor Plays Stoner and Serious." *USA Today*, August 4, 2008. www.usatoday.com/printedition/life/20080804/d_cover04_franco_cover.art.htm.
52. Kenneth Turan. "Review: 'Milk.'" *Los Angeles Times*, November 26, 2008. www.latimes.com/entertainment/la-et-milk26-2008nov26,0,5778683.story.
53. Quoted in Freydkin. "James Franco Digs Deep."
54. Quoted in *Morning Edition*. "James Franco Doesn't Limit Himself to Acting."
55. Quoted in Anderson. "The James Franco Project."
56. Quoted in Anderson. "The James Franco Project."
57. Quoted in Jamie Schram and Frank Rosario. "Professor Claims NYU Fired Him After He Gave James Franco a 'D.'" *New York Post*, December 19, 2011. www.nypost.com/p/news/local/manhattan/the_franco_cut_kIRVk4WuVdydz59WZ4I5tL.
58. John Williams. "What It's like to Be James Franco's Professor." *Slate*, December 20, 2011. www.slate.com/articles/arts/culturebox/2011/12/james_franco_at_yale_franco_s_professor_speaks_.single.html.
59. Williams. "What It's like to Be James Franco's Professor."
60. Anderson. "The James Franco Project."
61. Anderson. "The James Franco Project."
62. Quoted in Lisa Foderaro. "James Franco Straddles Two Roles at Yale." *New York Times.com*, March 3, 2011. www.nytimes.com/2011/03/04/nyregion/04franco.html.
63. Quoted in Anderson. "The James Franco Project."
64. Quoted in Cage. "James Franco."

65. Quoted in David Kamp. "Franco Cum Laude." *Vanity Fair*, December 2008. www.vanityfair.com/culture/features/2008/12/franco200812.

66. Quoted in Paul Chi. "James Franco Loves His New Role as a Professional Student." *People.com*, May 3, 2010. www.people.com/people/article/0,,20366041,00.html.

Chapter 4: Multitasking Franco

67. Karina Longworth. "James Franco's *Saturday Night Live* Doc: Unintentionally Fascinating." *LA Weekly*, March 14, 2010. http://blogs.laweekly.com/arts/2010/03/james_francos_saturday_night_l.php.

68. Sophia Lee. "L.A. Film Festival: James Franco Back to Esoterica in Another Turn as a Gay Poet." *Los Angeles Times*, June 21, 2011. http://latimesblogs.latimes.com/movies/2011/06/la-film-festival-james-franco-gay-poet-broken-tower.html.

69. Quoted in Lee. "L.A. Film Festival."

70. Quoted in Ryzik. "The (Extremely) Creative Ferment of James Franco."

71. Oscar Villalon. "James Franco's 'Palo Alto' Is a Cold, Empty Place—Except for the Weed." *San Francisco Weekly*, October 13, 2010. www.sfweekly.com/2010-10-06/culture/james-franco-s-palo-alto-is-a-cold-empty-place-except-for-the-weed.

72. Joshua Mohr. "Teen Spirit, Soured." *New York Times.com*, October 22, 2010. www.nytimes.com/2010/10/24/books/review/Mohr-t.html.

73. Quoted in *Charlie Rose*. "James Franco."

74. Quoted in Ryzik. "The (Extremely) Creative Ferment of James Franco."

75. Quoted in *All Things Considered*. "James Franco Checks In to 'General Hospital.'" National Public Radio, November 20, 2009. www.npr.org/templates/story/story.php?storyId=120566505.

76. James Franco. "A Star, a Soap, and the Meaning of Art." *Wall Street Journal*, December 4, 2009. http://online.wsj .com/article/SB100014240527487041071045745703133 72878136.html.

77. Franco. "A Star, a Soap, and the Meaning of Art."

78. Quoted in *Charlie Rose*. "James Franco."

79. Roberta Smith. "When an Actor Casts Himself as Artist." *New York Times.com*, August 19, 2010. www.nytimes .com/2010/08/20/arts/design/20franco.html.

80. Museum of Non-visible Art. "About." http://museumofnon-visibleart.com/about.

81. James Franco. "Museum of Non-visible Art—Praxis & James Franco Collaborate." Video. Kickstarter. www.kickstarter .com/projects/praxis/museum-of-non-visible-art-praxis -and-james-franco.

82. Annie Vaughan. "James Franco Makes Invisible Art He Sells for Real Money." Fox News.com, June 23, 2011. www .foxnews.com/entertainment/2011/06/23/james-franco -creates-invisible-art/#ixzz1kcfRxtvh.

83. Emma Mustich. "James Franco's Crazy New Art Project." *Salon.com*, June 13, 2011. www.salon.com/2011/06/13 /james_franco_museum.

84. Quoted in *Charlie Rose*. "James Franco."

Chapter 5: Who Is the Real James Franco?

85. Quoted in Andrea Mandell. "James Franco: Actor, Teacher, Explorer; And with His Plate So Full, the Guy's Single Again." *USA Today*, August 5, 2011. www.usatoday.com/LIFE /usaedition/2011-08-05-James-Franco-INSIDE_ST_U.htm.

86. Anderson. "The James Franco Project."

87. Quoted in Anderson. "The James Franco Project."

88. Quoted in Helen Pidd. "The Many Lives of James Franco." *Guardian* (UK), February 20, 2011. www.guardian.co.uk /artanddesign/2011/feb/20/james-franco-art-oscars-interview.

89. Quoted in Shone. "A Class Apart."

90. Quoted in Shone. "A Class Apart."

91. Quoted in Ryzik. "The (Extremely) Creative Ferment of James Franco."

92. Quoted in James Mottram. "James Franco: A Life in Constant Motion." *Independent* (UK), December 31, 2010. www.independent.co.uk/arts-entertainment/films/features/james-franco—a-life-in-constant-motion-2172395.html.

93. Quoted in Pidd. "The Many Lives of James Franco."

94. Quoted in Shone. "A Class Apart."

95. Quoted in Keith Staskiewicz. "James Franco on Playing Gay Characters: 'You Know What, Maybe I'm Just Gay.'" *EW.com*, January 5, 2011. http://insidemovies.ew.com/2011/01/05/james-franco-gay-roles.

96. Anderson. "The James Franco Project."

97. Quoted in Shone. "A Class Apart."

98. Quoted in Shone. "A Class Apart."

99. Bill Goodykoontz. "'127 Hours,' 4.5 Stars." *Arizona Republic*, November 17, 2010. www.azcentral.com/thingstodo/movies/articles/2010/11/17/20101117-days-review-goodykoontz.html.

100. A.O. Scott. "The Tale of a Shocking Fall and Gritty Resolve." *New York Times.com*, November 4, 2010. www.nytimes.com/2010/11/05/movies/05one.html.

101. Quoted in Andrea Mandell. "James Franco Goes 'Apes' over New Movie: Star Says the High-Tech Effects Sealed the Deal." *USA Today*, August 5, 2011. www.usatoday.com/life/people/2011-08-04-james-franco-rise-of-the-planet-of-the-apes_n.htm.

Important Dates

1978

James Edward Franco is born on April 19, 1978, in Palo Alto, California.

1996

Enrolls in UCLA to major in English.

1997

Drops out of UCLA and gets a job at a McDonald's restaurant to support himself while he begins taking classes at Playhouse West.

1999

Earns a role as Daniel Desario in a pilot for a television show called *Freaks and Geeks* that becomes a cult hit, though it was canceled after twelve episodes, although eighteen episodes were aired.

2001

Plays legendary Hollywood actor James Dean in a made-for-television biopic called *James Dean*, in which he used extreme method-acting techniques to get into character; the role earns him notice, a Golden Globe Award, Emmy and Screen Actors Guild Award nominations, and further auditions in Hollywood.

2002

Plays Harry Osborn in *Spider-Man*, a male gigolo named Sonny in the movie *Sonny*, and a homeless drug addict in the movie *City by the Sea*.

2003

Costars in Robert Altman's ballet movie, *The Company*.

2004

Reprises his role as Harry Osborn in *Spider-Man 2*.

2005

Has his directorial debut in *The Ape*, a dark comedy that he wrote with writing partner Merriwether Williams and starred in; stars in the war movie *The Great Raid*.

2006

Stars in *Tristan + Isolde*, *Annapolis*, and *Flyboys*; returns to UCLA as a full-time student, majoring in English with a concentration in creative writing.

2007

Reprises his role as Harry Osborn in *Spider-Man 3*.

2008

Stars in *Pineapple Express* as stoner Saul, and in *Milk* as Harvey Milk's boyfriend; graduates from UCLA and then moves to New York City for graduate school; concurrently enrolls in Columbia's MFA in creative writing program, NYU's filmmaking program, and Brooklyn College for another MFA in creative writing; hosts *Saturday Night Live* for the first time; returns to the show to film a documentary on the development of a single episode.

2009

Begins a recurring role as the demented artist Franco on the daytime soap opera *General Hospital*.

2010

Makes guest appearances as himself on the television show *30 Rock* and in the movie *Date Night*; has a small role in the movie *Eat, Pray, Love*; stars as poet Allen Ginsberg in the movie *Howl* and as mountain climber Aron Ralston in the movie *127 Hours*, earning rave reviews and a nomination for an Academy Award for Best Actor; opens an exhibit at the Museum of Contemporary

Art in Los Angeles based on his performance art experience playing Franco on *General Hospital*; graduates from Columbia's MFA program and enrolls in a PhD program at Yale University in New Haven, Connecticut; opens solo art show in New York City, called the *Dangerous Book Four Boys*; his book of short stories, *Palo Alto*, is published.

2011

Cohosts the Academy Awards alongside Anne Hathaway; costars with Natalie Portman in the movie *Your Highness*; stars in the movie *Rise of the Planet of the Apes* as scientist Will Rodman; makes and stars in *The Broken Tower*, a film about poet Hart Crane, and premieres the movie at the Los Angeles Film Festival; graduates from NYU's filmmaking school and begins taking classes in the digital and media department of RISD; teaches a class on adapting poetry to film in NYU's filmmaking program; co-founds the Museum of Non-Visible Art (MONA); collaborates with musician Kalup Linzy on several dance music tracks and a music video.

2012

Plays Hugh Hefner in a movie about Linda Lovelace called *Lovelace*.

For More Information

Books

James Franco. *Palo Alto*. New York: Scribner, 2010. This book of short stories features tales set in Franco's hometown of Palo Alto. Though the stories are fictional, many are based on Franco's memories of adolescence.

James Franco. *The Dangerous Book Four Boys*. New York: Rizzoli, 2012. This book features artwork from Franco's multimedia exhibit at the Clocktower Gallery in 2011. The show and resulting book explore themes of adolescence, nostalgia, and destruction.

Conn Iggulden and Hal Iggulden. *The Dangerous Book for Boys*. New York: Harper Collins, 2007. Franco based the title of his art exhibit on this book, which covers topics such as how to tie knots, build tree houses, and understand girls. Though the book addresses boyhood, the intended audience is eighteen and older.

Paul Mariani. *The Broken Tower: The Life of Hart Crane*. New York: Norton, 2000. Franco based his film about Hart Crane, his thesis project for NYU's filmmaking program, on this book.

Aron Ralston. *Between a Rock and a Hard Place*. London: Simon & Schuster, 2005. The movie *127 Hours* is based on the true story of this mountain climber, who in 2003 became trapped in a canyon while hiking alone. He saved his own life by cutting off his arm to free himself.

Randy Shilts. *The Mayor of Castro Street: The Life and Times of Harvey Milk*. New York: St. Martin's, 1982. A biography of San Francisco politician Harvey Milk. Franco played Scott Smith, Milk's boyfriend, in the critically acclaimed 2008 movie.

Periodicals

Sam Anderson. "The James Franco Project." *New York*, July 25, 2010. http://nymag.com/movies/profiles/67284.

Kate Bittman. "The Exchange: James Franco." *New Yorker*, November 3, 2010. www.newyorker.com/online/blogs /books/2010/11/the-exchange-james-franco.html.

Tom Chiarella. "James Franco Eight Ways." *Esquire*, September 2010. www.esquire.com/features/james-franco/james-franco -interview-0910#ixzz1kPvVuXAw.

James Franco. "A Star, a Soap, and the Meaning of Art." *Wall Street Journal*, December 4, 2009. http://online.wsj.com/article/SB10 0014240527487041071045745703133372878136.html.

Helen Pidd. "The Many Lives of James Franco." *Guardian* (UK), February 20, 2011. www.guardian.co.uk/artanddesign/2011 /feb/20/james-franco-art-oscars-interview.

Melena Ryzik. "James Franco's (Extremely) Creative Ferment." *New York Times.com*, September 8, 2010. www.nytimes .com/2010/09/12/movies/12ryzik.html?pagewanted=all.

Tom Shone. "A Class Apart: An Interview with James Franco." *Telegraph* (UK), January 4, 2011. www.telegraph.co.uk/culture /film/starsandstories/8209459/A-class-apart-interview-with -James-Franco.html.

Gus Van Sant. "James Franco." *Interview*, February 2010. www .interviewmagazine.com/film/james-franco/#_.

Internet Sources

Charlie Rose. "James Franco." Video. May 6, 2011. www.charlierose .com/view/interview/11661.

Ben Child. "James Franco and Kalup Linzy 'Turn It Up.'" *Guardian* (UK), July 13, 2011. www.guardian.co.uk/film/2011/jul/13 /james-franco-kalup-linzy-turn-it-up.

The Colbert Report. "James Franco Pt. 1." Video. Colbert Nation .com. April 5, 2011. www.colbertnation.com/the-colbert -report-videos/380445/april-05-2011/james-franco-pt--1.

Eric Ditzien. "James Franco on Embracing the Funny." *EW.com*, April 23, 2008. www.ew.com/ew/article/0,,20194235,00 .html.

Inside the Actors Studio. "James Franco: On Acting." Video. Bravo TV.com, December 7, 2010. www.bravotv.com/inside-the -actors-studio/season-17/videos/james-franco-on-acting.

Michelle King. "James Franco's Upcoming 'General Hospital' Appearance Explained." *Speakeasy* (blog), *Wall Street Journal*, November 6, 2009. http://blogs.wsj.com/speakeasy /2009/11/06/james-francos-upcoming-general-hospital -appearance-explained.

New York Times.com. "Screen Test: James Franco." Video. July 17, 2008. http://video.nytimes.com/video/2008/07/17/style /tmagazine/1194817109952/screen-test-james-franco.html?sc p=44&sq=James%20Franco&st=cse.

Emily Watkins. "Can You Afford to Live the Life of James Franco?" Vulture, February 10, 2011. www.vulture.com/2011/02/james_ franco_2.html.

John Williams. "What It's like to Be James Franco's Professor." *Slate*, December 20, 2011. www.slate.com/articles/arts /culturebox/2011/12/james_franco_at_yale_franco_s_ professor_speaks_.single.html.

Websites

Betsy Franco (www.betsyfranco.com). This website is maintained by author Betsy Franco, James Franco's mother. The site describes new books and projects and features a blog. Several pages include photos of Betsy Franco with her other famous family members.

Funny or Die (www.funnyordie.com/james_franco). This is the James Franco page on the comedy website Funny or Die. Franco has filmed a number of satirical videos such as *Acting with James Franco* for the website. He often chooses to make fun of himself or his projects on the website, and several of the videos are filmed with Franco's younger brother, Dave.

Harvey Milk Foundation (http://milkfoundation.org). This foundation, organized after Harvey Milk's assassination, spreads Milk's vision for a better world. Through a variety of programs, the foundation works to achieve equality for gay, lesbian, and transgendered individuals.

Museum of Non-visible Art (www.nonvisiblemuseum.com). James Franco helped found the Museum of Non-visible Art. Several pieces of his imagined artwork are described and for sale on this website.

Rabbit Bandini Productions (http://rabbitbandinifilms.com/index.html). The official site for the production company run by James Franco and his partner, Vince Jolivette.

Index

Picture Credits

About the Author

Christie Brewer Boyd lives in Ohio with her husband and daughter. She has written several titles in Lucent's People in the News series, including *Eminem* and *Nicki Minaj*.